The Constitution for the Federation of the Earth

The Constitution for the Federation of the Earth

The Institute for Economic Democracy

Constitution for the Federation of the Earth,
Compact Edition

ISBN 978-1-933567-52-5

Institute for Economic Democracy
PO Box 309, Appomattox VA 24522, USA.

Contents

Contents   v

Introduction by Glen T. Martin   1
     Old & New Paradigms   4
     Holism and the *Earth Constitution* . . .   15
     A Peace System   26
     A Prosperity System—The New
         Democratic Economics   36
     A Justice System   45
     A Freedom System   48
     A Sustainability System   53
     Conclusion   62
     Works Cited   65

Preamble   69

1   Broad Functions of the Earth Federation   71

2   **Basic Structure of the Earth Federation**   73

3   **Organs of the Earth Federation**   77

4   **Grant of Specific Powers**   79

5   **The World Parliament**   89
    Section 5.1   Functions and Powers . .   89
    Section 5.2   Composition   92
    Section 5.3   The House of Peoples   . .   93
    Section 5.4   The House of Nations   . .   93
    Section 5.5   The House of Counsellors   95
    Section 5.6   Procedures of the World
                  Parliament   96

6   **The World Executive**   101
    Section 6.1   Functions and Powers . .   101
    Section 6.2   Composition   103
    Section 6.3   The Presidium   103
    Section 6.4   The Executive Cabinet . .   105
    Section 6.5   Procedures   107
    Section 6.6   Limitations   109

7   **The World Administration**   111
    Section 7.1   Functions   111
    Section 7.2   Structure and Procedures   112
    Section 7.3   Departments   115

8   **The Integrative Complex**   119
    Section 8.1   Definition   119

Section 8.2   The World Civil Service
             Administration 121
Section 8.3   The World Boundaries
             andElections Administration . 122
Section 8.4   Institute on Governmen-
             tal Procedures and World
             Problems 126
Section 8.5   The Agency for Research
             and Planning 128
Section 8.6   Agency for Technologi-
             cal/Environmental Assessment 131
Section 8.7   The World Financial Ad-
             ministration 134
Section 8.8   Commission for Legistla-
             tive Review 138

9   The World Judiciary   141
Section 9.1   Jurisdiction of the World
             Supreme Court 141
Section 9.2   Benches of the World
             Supreme Court 142
Section 9.3   Seats of the World
             Supreme Court 145
Section 9.4   Collegium of World Judges 146
Section 9.5   The Superior Tribunal of
             World Supreme Court 149

10 The Enforcement System   151
Section 10.1   Basic Principles 151
Section 10.2   World Attorneys General 153
Section 10.3   The World Police 156

Section 10.4 The Means of Enforcement 157

11 The World Ombudsmus   **161**
   Section 11.1 Functions and Powers . .   161
   Section 11.2 Composition   164

12 Bill of Rights for the Citizens of Earth   **167**

13 Directive Principles for the Earth Federation   **171**

14 Safeguards and Reservations   **175**
   Section 14.1 Certain Safeguards . . .   175
   Section 14.2 Reservation of Powers .   177

15 World Federal Zones and World Capitals   **179**
   Section 15.1 Word Federal Zones . . .   179
   Section 15.2 The World Capitals . . .   180
   Section 15.3 Locational Procedures . .   181

16 World Territories and Exterior Relations   **183**
   Section 16.1 World Territory   183
   Section 16.2 Exterior Relations 185

17 Ratification and Implementation   **187**
   Section 17.1 Ratification of the World
                 Constitution 187
   Section 17.2 Stages of Implementation   191
   Section 17.3 First Operative Stage of
                 World Government 192

Section 17.4   Second Operative Stage
    of World Government 199
Section 17.5   Full Operative Stage of
    World Government 205
Section 17.6   Costs of Ratification . . . 208

18 Amendments **211**
Section 18.1   211
Section 18.2   212
Section 18.3   212
Section 18.4   212
Section 18.5   213
Section 18.6   213

19 Provisional World Government **215**
Section 19.1   Actions to be Taken by
    the World Constituent Assembly 215
Section 19.2   Work of the Preparatory
    Commissions 217
Section 19.3   Composition of the Pro-
    visional World Parliament . . . 220
Section 19.4   Formation of the Provi-
    sional World Executive 222
Section 19.5   First Actions of the Pro-
    visional World Government . . 223

Additional Information **226**
Earth Federation Organizational Chart 226
Signatures 228
Pledge of Allegiance 244
World Constitution & Parliament Assoc. 245

Introduction

by Glen T. Martin

The 20th century produced what may well be the most important document for the 21st century and the future of human civilization: the *Constitution for the Federation of Earth*. In this introduction, I hope to illuminate the truth of this statement and to show why a decent future, even a possible future, for humanity almost certainly involves ratification of the *Earth Constitution* or some document very much like it. The *Constitution* can serve as a practical, common sense guide to establishing a decent planetary civilization (for the first time in history) of peace, prosperity, justice, freedom, and sustainability.

The *Constitution* was created through a dynamic process including hundreds, perhaps thousands, of world citizens meeting in four constituent assemblies in various cities of the world in 1968, 1977, 1979, and 1991, and communicating with one another regularly in between concerning the content of the emerging document. It had a central drafting committee of 25 persons and was primarily written by five persons, all experts in international law, world citizenship, and human affairs. I have described this process in detail in my introductions to *Constitution for the Federation of Earth: With Historical Introduction, Commentary, and Conclusion* (2010) and in my *The Earth Federation Movement: History, Documents, Philosophical Foundations* (2011). Even though other suggested constitutions have been written for the Earth, none have developed through this kind of worldwide dynamic participation, and none even approach the surpassing brilliance in conception and holistic integration of the *Earth Constitution*.

Since the fourth Constituent Assembly in Troia, Portugal, in 1991, the *Constitution* has been considered a completed document ready for ratification by the people of Earth under the democratic criteria set forth in Article 17. The framers considered it necessary to present it to the people of Earth as a finished document rather than continue a process of endless squabbling over details while our planet descends ever-more deeply into war, chaos, and environmental collapse. Article 19 of the *Constitution* empowers the people of Earth to begin Provisional World Government even before the process of ratification has been completed. Such is the seriousness of the emergency posed for our planet by proliferation of weapons of mass destruction, international chaos, multinational corporate greed, and planetary climate collapse. The World Constitution and Parliament Association (WCPA), founded by Philip and Margaret

Isely and others in 1958, has, from then to the present, sponsored the writing of the *Constitution*, the process of ratification, and the development of provisional world government.

The 20th century was a century of vast transformations in the understanding of our human situation. Out of its dynamic energy emerged one technological revolution after another: in an on-going process that appears to have no end in sight as we moved into the 21st century. Secondly, out of its tragic history of worldwide wars, genocides, and crimes against humanity emerged an understanding that *something is terribly wrong with civilization* as manifested in the 20th century, something that must be corrected if we are to survive much longer on this planet. Finally, from the dimension of the sciences, both the natural and the social sciences, emerged a new holistic scientific paradigm that superseded the older Newtonian paradigm of the early-modern period. This new paradigm has yet to be actualized in human civilization. It is embodied in the *Constitution for the Federation of Earth*. The *Constitution*, along with the work of the Provisional World Parliament under its authority, can be found at www.worldproblems.net or www.worldparliament-gov.org.

Old & New Paradigms

The older paradigm was predicated on assumptions about the universe as mechanistic, materialistic, atomistic, and reductionistic, assumptions that inevitably influenced our human philosophical self-understanding, leading, we shall see, to the vast cataclysms of war and destruction that pervaded the 20th century as well as to the on-going destruction of nature and our planetary environment. The universe was seen as a collection of impersonal forces and laws operating within a universal causal determinism. These forces and laws left no intelligible place for human consciousness, spirituality, morality, or religion. It appeared that humans were estranged within an impersonal and implacable world system built up mechanistically from its atomistic substructure, within which objects and forces had only *external* relationships with one another. The world, in this sense, was inherently fragmented: diverse forces, atomistically conceived, with merely external relationships to other such forces.

Two major civilizational components that seemed to correctly mirror these premises developed out of the Renaissance and came to dominate all human relationships: the system of sovereign nation-states integrated with the system of global capitalism. Both systems appeared to correctly derive from early-modern scientific assumptions. It was assumed as 'natural' that human beings would live within territorially bounded, militarized states in external relationships with one another that resulted in diplomatic and strategic maneuvering vis-à-vis one another and occasionally in war. As G.W.F. Hegel put it in his early 19th century *Philosophy of Right*:

> The nation state is the spirit in its substantial rationality and immediate actuality, and is therefore the absolute power on *earth*; each state is consequently a sovereign and independent entity in relation to others. There is no Praetor to adjudicate between States, but at most arbitrators and mediators, and even the presence of these will be contingent, i.e., determined by particular wills. ... Consequently, if no agreement can be reached between the particular wills, conflicts between states can only be settled by war. ... (1991, pars. 331, 333-334)

Similarly capitalism understood human life as composed of rationally self-interested individuals who, both individually and collectively through their businesses and corporations, competed with one another for the accumulation of profit in the service of satisfaction of their unlimited desires. The theory stated that free competition among this (atomistic) multiplicity would result in the greatest efficiency and maximum production of goods and services necessary to human flourishing. Adam Smith termed this promised result 'the invisible hand'—many individuals competing in the market-place out of pure self-interest would produce the greatest good for the greatest number of persons. Self-interested individuals and corporations stood basically in external relationships to one another: strategically maneuvering vis-à-vis one another and occasionally economically destroying one another in the competitive struggle (economic warfare).

Just as nations (as Hegel points out) although made up of millions of persons, act as 'particular wills' in external relations that struggle strategically and may wind up in war, so corporations, although employing many persons, are run by a CEO or tiny CEO group representing the investors who act as 'particular wills' (bosses over many employees who obey their orders) in external relations that struggle strategically and may wind up in economic warfare. The system of autonomous nation-states operates on very similar assumptions to the economic system of autonomous individuals and corporations. And in fact, these institutions have always operated and worked together, each nation-state promoting its own perceived economic interests through the promotion of its private businesses at home and world-

wide, diplomatically and militarily. As social
scientist Christopher Chase-Dunn puts it:

> The state and the interstate system are
> not separate from capitalism, but rather
> are the main institutional supports of
> capitalist production relations. The sys-
> tem of unequally powerful and com-
> peting nation-states is part of the com-
> petitive struggle of capitalism, and thus
> wars and geopolitics are a systematic
> part of capitalist dynamics, not exoge-
> nous forces. (1998: 61)

Are the immense and continuous wars, genocides, and crimes against humanity of the 20th
century connected with these two dominant institutions deriving from early modern assumptions? Philosopher Nolan Pliny Jacobson con-
cludes that "the major source of retardation
endangering the future planetary civilization
about which so much has been written...*is the
kind of selfhood in which the terrors of the modern nation are rooted. It is the archaic legacy of a
self-substance, mutually independent of all others,
which supports the entire superstructure of West-
ern nations*" (1982: 41). Jacobson refers to a na-
tionalistic selfhood that is expressed in 'particular wills' facing one another in strategic and
external relationships, the final result of which
is ultimately war. In just the same way, under capitalism, corporations function as a form

of collective selfhood understood as 'particular wills' in external relationships, locked in struggles for profit and ascendency. This outmoded and lethal paradigm continues to dominate human civilization, endangering our future, and even the future of life on our planet.

The new paradigm arising from both the social and natural sciences centers around *holism*—wholes within wholes and fields within fields (not atomistically conceived fragments) constitute the basic structure of the universe, our planetary ecology, and human life. From systems theory to social scientific understandings of sociology and psychology to macroscopic and microscopic physics—across the entire conceptual landscape, it has been recognized that wholes are prior to parts and these wholes integrate the parts into dynamic systems in which the parts flourish in a set of *internal* relationships to one another. Internal relationships mean the parts are not autonomous atoms apart from the systems within which they are both constituted and embedded. Rather, the parts are interdependent and interrelated in a multiplicity of ways conditioned by the principle of the wholes of which they are part.

This is not the place to undertake a scholarly documentation of the new holism of the social and natural sciences. I have already done this in such works as *Ascent to Freedom* (2008), *Triumph of Civilization* (2010) and *The Earth Fed-*

eration Movement (2011). A few brief quotes will suffice to indicate the conceptual foundations of the *Earth Constitution*—quotes from social sciences, from life-sciences (ecology), and from contemporary physics. Psychoanalyst and philosopher Erich Fromm writes:

> We consider people to be "religious" because they say they believe in God. Is there any difficulty in saying this? Is there any reality in it, except that the words are uttered? Obviously I am speaking here about an experience which should constitute the reality behind the words. What is this experience? It is one of recognizing oneself as part of humanity, of living according to a set of values in which the full experience of love, justice, truth, is the dominant goal of life to which everything else is subordinated; it means a constant striving to develop one's powers of life and reason to a point at which a new harmony with the world is attained; it means striving for humility, to see one's identity with all beings, and to give up the illusion of a separate, indestructible ego. (1962: 156)

Fromm's language is strikingly similar to that of Jacobson, quoted above. Human beings emerged into self-consciousness during the Axial Period in human history (8th to 2nd cen-

tury BCE) and more acutely so during the Renaissance of the 15th and 16th centuries. This
emergence of self-awareness resulted in a grow-
ing sense of autonomy, of personal separate-
ness from nature and the rest of humanity. 'The
illusion of a separate, indestructible ego' be-
came fundamental to both sovereign nation-
states (collective egos) and personal economic
life under capitalism (competitive rationally
self-interested egos). But our task, for Fromm,
is precisely to overcome this illusion and discover a new harmony with humanity and nature. 'God,' for him, is a symbol of that whole-
ness and harmony. To be religious is to be concerned with all others in a relationship of *agape*,
as emphasized in Christianity, or *karuna*, as emphasized in Buddhism. Jesus understands God
as saying to humanity: "When you have done
it unto the least of these my brethren you have
done it unto me" (Matt. 25:40). The harmony is
really there in the pervasive holism of existence
and can be recognized if we give up the illusion
of a separate ego.

Advanced psychology and sociology today
understand that individuals are not prior to, nor
independent from, society, other persons, or humanity as a whole. Our relations with others are
internal—our personhood as well as our well-
being are functions of the whole. Individual and
whole arise together—there are no wholes without parts and no parts without wholes that con-

stitute them and condition their nature. *Unity in diversity* is the principle of holism. Parts are not denied but understood as deeply (internally) related to the wholes of which they are parts. This is not only the view of advanced psychology and sociology, it is also the view of advanced physics. The holism of the universe has been discovered (since Einstein's special and general theories of relativity that appeared in 1905 and 1915), and this holism includes human life. As scientific cosmologist Milton K. Munitz puts this: "The universe and human life are coupled. If we are to understand either, we need to move in both directions: from the universe to man and from man to the universe, since they are mutually involved in a very special way"(1986: 237). Physicist Henry Stapp writes:

> The scientific task of explicating this general quantum-mechanical ontology is just beginning. But even the general features of the quantum ontology involve a conception of man and nature profoundly different from the picture provided by classical physics. For man appears no longer as an isolated automaton. He appears rather as an integral part of the highly nonlocal creative activity of the universe. The revision of the conception of a person, and of his perceived relation to the rest of nature, cannot help but have an immense impact on what is

perceived as valuable. It must inevitably
lead us away from the egocentric bias
that was the rational product of the on-
tology of classical physics, to the values
inherent in the image of self, not as a
local isolated automaton but rather as a
nonlocalizable integrated aspect of the
creative impulse of the universe. (Henry
Stapp, 1988, 57)

Again, Stapp sees our 'egocentric bias' as
a product of the older paradigm of classical
physics. Human beings are no longer understood as alienated strangers in a mechanistic
and impersonal cosmos. We are an 'integrated
aspect of the creative impulse of the universe'
itself. Holism pervades all things and the parts
are integral to the series of wholes that encompass and condition them. The same principle
applies in biology and ecology. In his 1996 book
*The Web of Life: A New Scientific Understand-
ing of Living Systems*, Fritjof Capra expresses the
holism now understood by contemporary sciences: "Interdependence—the mutual depen-
dence of all life processes on one another—is
the nature of all ecological relationships. The
behavior of every living member of the ecosystem depends on the behavior of many others.
The success of the whole community depends
on the success of its individual members, while
the success of each member depends on the success of the community as a whole" (298). In

their book, *The Liberation of Life*, Charles Birch
and John B. Cobb, Jr. characterize 'the ecological model' and point out that this model is also
a corollary of contemporary holistic physics:

> The ecological model proposes that
> on closer examination the con-
> stituent elements of the structure at
> each level operate in patterns of in-
> terconnectedness which are not me-
> chanical. Each element behaves as
> it does because of the relations it
> has to other elements in the whole,
> and these relations are not well
> understood in terms of the laws
> of mechanics. The true charac-
> ter of these relations is discussed
> in the following section as 'inter-
> nal' relations.... Internal relations
> characterize events. For example,
> field theory in physics shows that
> the events which make up the field
> have their existence only as parts of
> the field. These events cannot exist
> apart from the field. They are inter-
> nally related to one another. (1990:
> 83 & 88)

It is the lack of operating from these internal relationships by contemporary nation-states
and capitalist 'free markets' that is playing such

havoc with peaceful human relationships and
the biosphere of our planet. In economics we
operate according to so called 'natural laws' of
the market regardless of who gets hurt economically in terms of the poverty of vast sections
of humanity and regardless of the consequences
for our planet's biosphere. As Chris Williams
expresses this: "capitalism is thus systematically driven toward the ruination of the planet
and we underestimate how committed the system is to planetary ecocide at our peril. As
stated above, ecological devastation is just as intrinsic to the operation of capitalism as is the
exploitation of the vast majority of humans in
the interests of a tiny minority, imperialism, and
war" (2010: 232).

The paradigm-shift to holism would necessarily mean devising an economic system
premised on the reasonable interdependent
prosperity of all rather than the appropriation
of super-riches for the few at the expense of the
vast majority. It would mean devising an economic system recognizing that we live within
a finite, delicately balanced biosphere, in which
resource and energy extractions from nature, as
well as waste and heat externalities at the other
end of the economic process, must conform to
that finitude and ecological balance (cf. Daly
1996). It would also necessarily mean the end of
the war-system and the industrial-military complex that profits from that system, for war is

supremely destructive not only of human well-being but devastating for the environment.

The older fragmented and mechanistic assumptions about human life embodied in the system of autonomous, militarized nation-states and the economics of atomistic self-interest unconcerned with the consequences for the whole must be abandoned if we are to survive much longer on this planet. They must be replaced by a civilizational holism in which nations recognize their internal relations with all other nations and with humanity, and in which economics is predicated on this same recognition. We are all in this together. As Immanuel Kant already expressed this in the 18th century: "Because a (narrower or wider) community widely prevails among the Earth's peoples, a transgression of rights in *one* place in the world is felt *everywhere*" (1983: 119)

Holism and the *Earth Constitution*

The Preamble to the *Earth Constitution* provides the conceptual framework for the whole of the document. It gives us the language of a "new world which promises to usher in an era of peace, prosperity, justice and harmony." Given the bleak and bloody history of humankind to date, how can the framers of the *Constitution* be so confident? The answer is given in the second paragraph of the Preamble: "Aware of the interdependence of people, nations, and all life." This is a declaration of holism that could not be clearer: there is no such thing as autonomous independence from the rest of humanity, from the other nations of the world, or from the natural world.

The *Earth Constitution* is predicated throughout on this principle of unity in diversity based on awareness of the interdependence of all people and all life on Earth. Every agency or branch of the government established under the *Constitution* (from the World Parliament, the World Judiciary, the World Administration, and the World Police to the World Ombudsmus) is designed for a maximum of diversity, drawing its leadership from all continents and administrative regions of the world. Every agency or branch of government is structured to work harmoniously with all the others. At the same time, the government under the *Constitution* is designed so that power is dispersed and democratized widely. The Administrative or Executive branch has no police or military powers; all branches are responsible to the diverse World Parliament (composed of three houses, each very diverse in membership); the Ombudsmus is responsible to watch all the other branches, ensuring democratic operation and protection of human rights. The *Constitution* is brilliantly designed for maxim diversity within a unity of democratic principles of freedom, peace, sustainability and prosperity. It presents humanity with a holistic system that alone can end war and ground a sustainable and humane economic system.

The next four paragraphs in the Preamble address the consequences of the older fragmented paradigm: we are at the "brink of ecological and social catastrophe"; we are aware of the "total illusion" of "security through military defense"; we are aware of the terrible consequences of the global economic system that causes "ever increasing disparity between rich and poor"; and we are aware that we need to save humanity "from imminent and total annihilation." All these are caused by the older, dysfunctional world system of autonomous sovereign nation-states and a flawed, class-controlled economic system operating in coordination with this nation-state system. The outmoded paradigm of our current world disorder is leading our civilization to omnicide. The seventh paragraph of the Preamble again returns to the new paradigm announced in paragraph two:

> Conscious that Humanity is One despite the existence of diverse nations, races, creeds, ideologies and cultures and that the principle of unity in diversity is the basis for a new age when war shall be

outlawed and peace prevail; when the
earth's total resources shall be equitably
used for human welfare; and when basic
human rights and responsibilities shall
be shared by all without discrimination.

The statement of holism from paragraph two
is here spelled out in greater detail. The "diverse nations, races, creeds, ideologies and cultures" of the world no longer mean incom-
mensurable fragmentation, war, and conflict.
They are united within this *Constitution* under a
"principle of unity in diversity" that is the basis
for this "new age" of peace, justice, protection
of rights, and assumption of mutual universal
responsibilities by the people of Earth. The integrated ability of the Earth Federation government to deal with climate crisis and establishing world peace must be understood in terms of
this fundamental paradigm-shift from fragmentation to holism.

It is important to point out that the Preamble expresses its holism (correctly) as the "principle of unity in diversity." The scientific revolution that has placed holism at the center of all
processes within the universe understands that
a holistic system is qualitatively different from
a system of fragmented autonomous parts. In a
holistic system the unity in diversity means that
the whole functions well because of the parts
and the parts function well because of their in-

tegration into the whole. The uniqueness of the parts (diversity) is absolutely essential to the proper functioning of the whole. Throughout the universe, and throughout the ecosystems of the Earth, there are no wholes without diverse interacting parts. It is the same with the holism of the Earth Federation government under the *Earth Constitution*, the whole is systematically designed, as we shall see, to be the function of a diversity of interacting parts. In this government, there is simply no whole without these diverse parts. An integrated human community is assured.

There is an analogy with the power of health, for example, in a human body when all the organs are functioning and integrated into a harmonious whole. Parts and whole working cooperatively together create health in living things, in natural systems, and in the planetary ecosystem. Fragmentation in all these dimensions means death. Similarly, social fragmentation means war and violence, domination and exploitation. The power generated by social holism and world-system holism transforms these negative consequences into a synergistic flourishing of the whole with the harmonious integration of all its parts. This is what social power is and should be—the power of a genuine human community. The democratic function of the human community as the integration of unity in diversity will reflect the same holism that we seek to preserve for the biosphere of the Earth.

The commonly reproduced diagram of the Earth Federation government reveals the Earth Federation designed as an integrated and comprehensive system for preserving and actualizing this holism. The central authority in the world will be the World Parliament, made up of three houses. First is the House of Peoples, elected from 1000 electoral districts worldwide and soliciting the democratic participation of the peoples of Earth in operations of the Earth Federation. The Provisional World Parliament has also created the "Global Peoples Assembly" as part of the World Elections Act (WLA 29) to further involve and empower grass roots participation in the Earth Federation government. To effectively prevent climate collapse and restore the environment it will be absolutely necessary to involve local citizens worldwide in the process of conversion to a sustainable way of living.

Second is the House of Nations, with 1, 2, or 3 representatives from each nation depending on population. The concept of 'nationhood' will not have the kind of lethal life or death connotation that it currently has among the 193, mostly militarized, sovereign entities today. Under the *Earth Constitution*, it will be easy to create new nations (depending on people's desires) for minorities or other groups who wish a measure of local self-government. Third, and absolutely vital to the holism of the *Earth Constitution*, is the House of Counsellors (200 representatives from 20 global regions) whose job will be to serve as a source of expertise (including expertise on sustainability, democracy, human rights, ecology, etc.) for the Parliament and to represent the *whole* of the Earth and its interests within the World Parliament.

Sessions of the World Parliament may rotate among the five world capitals to be established on five continents. Every continent, nation, and grouping is to be included. The continents of the world are further divided into ten magna-regions (primarily according to population) and twenty administrative regions. Many appointments require a representative from each of these regions, or from each continental division, assuring a continual, and continually variable, diversity filling the high posts of government.

At its first session, each house of the Parliament will elect a panel of five chairpersons, one from each continent, who will rotate annually as chair of that house, the other four serving as vice-chairs each year (Art.5.6.1). Similarly, the Presidium that manages the World Executive branch of the government will consist of five persons, one from each continental division. These five will rotate annually as the President, with the others serving as vice-presidents each year. Similarly, the Executive Cabinet under the Presidium will be composed of twenty to thirty members with at least one from each of the ten administrative magna-regions of the world and with no more than two members from any one nation.

The principle of unity in diversity, reflected in this system of appointments, will also apply to appointments for the World Attorney's General who, with the World Police, will be responsible for enforcement of Earth Federation laws worldwide. The office of the World Attorney's General will again be run by five members, one from each continental division, with the five rotating in the position of World Attorney General every two years. Similarly, the twenty Regional Attorney Generals will be elected from each of the twenty federal administrative regions of the world system, guaranteeing representation from every part of the planet.

Exactly the same structure applies to the office of the World Ombudsmus. The office will be run by five World Ombudsmen, one from each continental division, who will rotate to the office of Principle World Ombudsman every two years. As with the World Attorneys General, there will be twenty world regional offices run by World Advocates under this office, each elected from one of the twenty federal world regions. The fourth office directly responsible to the World Parliament is the World Judiciary, structured within a Collegium of World Judges numbering up to 60 judges, with an equal number elected from each of the ten magna-regions of the world federal administrative districts. Each of the main branches of the Earth Federation, therefore, including the World Parliament, will be structured according to this principle of unity in diversity to ensure that interdependent diversity is the empowering principle behind the holism.

The *Constitution* sets up a series of seven agencies called the Integrative Complex to serve the functioning of all aspects of the Earth Federation government. The research, knowledge, assessment, and planning capacities of these agencies will be drawn upon by all the other organs of the Earth Federation, hence "integrating" the knowledge and functioning of the diverse departments and branches of the government. One fundamental way to deal with the series of global crises identified in the Preamble and Article 1 of the *Constitution* is to establish an integrated, diverse, and smoothly functioning world system directed toward addressing these crises in an efficient and holistic manner.

That is the conceptual basis of the *Earth Constitution*. It institutionalizes peace, prosperity, justice, freedom, and sustainability for the people of Earth. Let us look at how this is done within each category. A model of the world system created by the *Constitution* and based on these five categories was passed as an official document at the 12th session of the Provisional World Parliament in Kolkata, India, December 2011. It was written and introduced to the Parliament by the present author. Within each category, the work of the Provisional World Parliament is integrated with exposition of the holism of the *Earth Constitution*. This document is published as part of my book *The Earth Federation Movement* (2011).The exposition below provides an abbreviated version of this document for each category, which may well serve as the most adequate brief introduction to the *Earth Constitution*.

To understand the deep significance of paradigms consider the 14th century ideas concerning physics. Only six centuries ago, even the most intelligent people believed that the world was composed of four basic elements: earth, air, fire, and water. The lowest element and closest to the center of the created world was earth. Earth, and all things made of earth (in general, physical objects) naturally tend to the center. If you hold up an object and drop it, it falls back to the earth because it is naturally tending toward the center. The elements formed a hierarchy, beginning with earth as the lowest, and ascending toward God, with fire as the highest of the four before the divine element of the 'ether' (the 'fifth element') of which the sun, moon, and heavenly bodies were composed. The social consequences of this paradigm resulted in the hierarchical social and economic systems that characterized medieval feudalism.

Within a couple of centuries, early modern science had entirely overthrown this paradigm and established another physics that we described above—a mechanistic and atomistic physics of impersonal forces that could find no conceptual place for human dignity, spirituality, or ethical aspirations. Out of this early-modern paradigm came the impersonal, fragmented social systems of 'free market' capitalism and militarized, autonomous nation-states. We have examined above the inevitable consequences of these social and economic systems in terms of war, poverty, domination, exploitation, and destruction of nature. Conceptual models of the way things work are institutionalized into social systems, and these systems have predictable consequences.

In the 20th century scientists uncovered another paradigm that revealed the errors of early-modern physics. The new paradigm was holistic, superseding atomism and fragmentation, and opening the possibility for a reintegration of human dignity, spirituality, and ethical aspirations into our understanding of the whole. It was an *emergent evolutionary paradigm* showing human development through the process of evolution and a progressive human self-understanding throughout history. This new paradigm was integrated into the *Earth Constitution* that can new serve as a foundation for new social and economic systems on the Earth. Just as former social and economic systems had consequences, so the new system will have consequences. And these can be predicted with some certainty given a clear understanding of the paradigm from which they derive and how this is embodied in the *Earth Constitution*.The consequences of the new system under the *Constitution* will be a significant worldwide increase in peace, prosperity, justice, freedom, and sustainability. (The following sections draw from my book *The Earth Federation Movement*, 2011.)

A Peace System

Historically, many thinkers from the 17th century to the present have understood the world system of militarized sovereign nation-states as inherently a *war system*. War is not an occasional failure of this system but an intrinsic characteristic of the fact that there is no enforceable world law over nations and national leaders that can mandate demilitarization and bring to justice those who violate the peaceful democratic rule of law. In consequence, nations operate on the basis of power politics involving the implicit or explicit use of coercion to promote their variety of perceived self-interests. The result is a world of chaos, injustice, and violence that today wastes more than one trillion US dollars per year on militarism while the basic needs of the majority of human beings remain unmet. The result is a collection of 193 more or less autonomous entities who structurally deny our basic interdependence on this Earth and who utterly lack the ability to join together sufficiently to deal with global crises such as climate crisis, worldwide diminishing resources, or increasing global poverty.

People say war cannot be eliminated, and this is truly so under the institutionalized paradigm within which the world remains currently trapped. However, under the *Constitution*, the nations of the Earth Federation are federated under the common rule of enforceable laws. Sovereignty (delegated from the people of Earth) is shared by governmental authorities from the local to the national to the world level. The most fundamental component for creating a world peace system is *global democracy itself*, for democracy institutionalizes processes of nonviolent change and embraces all citizens within a regime of political participation within which their voices are heard and their rights are protected.

At the global level such a regime would abolish the fragmentation of militarized sovereign nation-states in lethal and secretive competition with one another while mitigating the fragmented identifications of people worldwide with their local religion, ethnicity, race, culture, or other groupings. Non-military global democracy would also eliminate the military-industrial complex in which tremendous profits are made from producing munitions and military machines and which promotes overwhelming incentives for war and perpetual violence.

For this reason the World Parliament created under the *Constitution* is the first and foremost component of a *world peace system*. The House of Peoples represents all people on Earth through representatives elected from 1000 electoral districts worldwide apportioned according to population. The House of Nations represents all nations with one to three representatives (depending on population) appointed or elected by the nations themselves. And the House of Councilors (composed of 200 representatives, 10 from each of 20 magna-regions worldwide) represents the people of Earth as a whole and the common good for the entire planet.

The world democracy created under the World Parliament composed of these three houses, therefore, will embrace all races, religions, and other groupings in global dialogue and decision-making. The House of Nations will embrace all nations large and small, ending imperialism and exploitation of weaker nations by powerful nations. And the House of Counselors, with experts on all aspects of our civilization from the environment to demilitarization to cultural conflicts to principles of sustainable development, will provide wisdom and expertise to the Parliament in the service of the common good of humanity and the planet.

The *Earth Constitution* converts today's system of fragmented individualism (of nations, corporations, and persons) to a *global social contract*. A global social contract means that all are included in the regime of collective empowerment. A planetary community is established on fundamental moral and practical principles thereby transforming (for many at least) self-interested individuals into responsible citizens. A truly democratic world system is an essential foundation stone for world peace. Every group and nation must feel that its voice is heard and that it may effectively participate in governing the Earth in cooperation with other world citizens throughout the Earth Federation. The establishment of an effective World Parliament alone creates the foundations for a genuine world peace system.

Second, under both the *Constitution* and the Provisional World Parliament, many specific features of the *Constitution* and laws passed by the Parliament establish the concrete lineaments of a world peace system. Not only does the *Earth Constitution* require a demilitarized world (beginning with its second stage of ratification), the Provisional World Parliament has created detailed legislation to regulate and empower the process of disarmament. The very

first World Legislative Act adopted in 1982 by
the Provisional World Parliament (WLA #1) enacted a world law prohibiting the design, development, sale, transport, or deployment of
weapons of mass destruction, including nuclear
weapons and the missiles that deliver them.

A number of scholars have pointed out that
private terrorism is simply war by another
name. It is war waged by the weak and rel-
atively powerless as opposed to war financed
and organized by nation-states (state terrorism)
and their imperial military systems. The Provisional World Parliament, at its Second Session
in New Delhi, India, enacted WLA #8, creating
a World Commission on Terrorism. This commission is charged not only to invite cooperation from nations and NGOs in dealing with terrorism, it is also charged to address the fundamental causes of terrorism in terms of the per-
ceptions of gross injustices, the feeling of voice-
lessness among marginalized peoples, and the
perception that the current world political authorities are engaged in their own terrorist war
against certain groups, religions, or cultures.

The Parliament recognizes that we cannot
create a decent world order with ever more war
and violence, even if this is directed toward ter-
rorists and their organizations. Only changing
our institutional assumptions can change the
world order in meaningful ways. The peace system created by the *Earth Constitution* includes a

multiplicity of elements working together to ensure that the system establishes enduring peace. First and foremost, we have seen, is the establishment of *effective world democracy itself*, in which people and nations from the entire planet participate in governing the planet and thereby institutionalizing the procedures for nonviolent and peaceful social change. Today's sovereign nation-state system, with its militarism and national security apparatus, defeats authentic democracy in all nations. Authentic democracy can only develop in a demilitarized world recognizing *universal* rights, duties, freedoms, and obligations.

Third, the *Constitution* sets up an effective and impartial World Judiciary with authority over all persons, including national leaders. This ensures peace from two directions: all national leaders can be indicted for violating the law (no more impunity as in today's world) and a judiciary treating everyone fairly and equally under the law diminishes the feelings of resentment that now fuel much violence and war worldwide. The World Court system has eight benches designed to deal with the variety of cases that might endanger world peace. It has benches for human rights cases, for criminal cases dealing with individuals, corporations, or groups, for public cases dealing with conflict between government and corporations or other groups, and for international conflicts between nations. World peace through world law requires an effective judiciary to deal with all forms of conflict between individuals, groups, or nations. When people see impartial justice being done on a global scale, they will understand that a peace system has truly come into the world.

Fourth, the *Constitution* creates the Earth Federation Enforcement System of the world police and world attorneys general to ensure a peaceful and nonviolent world order premised on justice and the effective enforcement of the laws against war and violence everywhere on Earth. The police will possess only weapons necessary to apprehend individuals (Article 10.1.5). All weapons of war are abolished even for the Earth Federation Government. Both Articles 2 and 10 specify that the Earth Federation will be non-military. Article 10 specifies that one of the basic functions of the enforcement system will be "conflict resolution" and states that "a basic condition for preventing outbreaks of violence, which the Enforcement System shall facilitate in every way possible, shall be to assure a fair hearing under nonviolent circumstances for any person or group having a grievance, and likewise to assure a fair opportunity for a just settlement of any grievance with due regard for the rights and welfare of all concerned."

One branch of the World Police under the *Constitution* will be a Department of Conflict

Resolution. Officials in this department will not be allowed to carry any weapons nor do any undercover work and, according to to Provisional World Parliament legislation, they must be servants and facilitators of the people locally to solve and resolve their own problems. Nothing like this is found on a planetary scale in today's militarized global war system. This is truly what a peace system for the Earth will look like. People are empowered to create peace by an Earth Federation whose mission is to serve the people of Earth through a world system founded on peace, prosperity, justice, freedom, and sustainability. The emerging Earth Federation is an integrated whole with all these basic functions integrated into a practical and effective system of democratic world government.

Fifth, the *Constitution* creates another worldwide organization answering to the World Parliament that is a vital component of the world peace system: the World Ombudsmus. This organization, with offices everywhere within the Federation, will be devoted to protecting the human rights of the citizens of Earth (as specified in Articles 12 and 13) from violation by individuals, corporations, nations, or the World Government itself. The *Earth Constitution* recognizes so-called "third generation rights" of the right to peace and the right to a protected and decent environment. If people's rights, freedoms, peaceful coexistence, and planetary environment are really protected, the causes of war will be largely eliminated. The Ombudsmus constitutionally will have significant authority to act on behalf of the citizens of Earth to protect their many rights and freedoms identified by Articles 12 and 13. No nation or group will likely want to resort to violence when they see that their voices, dignity, and self-determination are respected and protected.

Sixth, the Provisional World Parliament passed a World Education Act (WLA #26) at its eighth session in Lucknow, India, in 2004. The Earth Federation government will promote high quality education everywhere and require all schools that are recipient of Earth Federation aid to include programs focusing on global issues, peace studies issues, study of the *Earth Constitution*, and study of the nature and responsibilities of good government within a global democracy. Education worldwide will promote peace, mutual tolerance, the founding principle of unity in diversity, and the dynamics of conflict resolution. Pedagogy will become a fundamental component in the world peace system.

Education will be one central component of an integrated Earth Federation plan to empower all citizens of the Earth to think in terms of the principle of unity in diversity, of mutual respect and tolerance within the framework of effective global democracy, and an educated citizenry capable of global citizenship. The Parliament un-

derstands that peace will be the product of a
global system with many components working
together: from good leadership, to the content
and attitude of the mass media, to the spirit and
intent with which corporations operate, to the
sense that people have of world citizenship, to
the degree of fairness and prosperity apparent
in the world, to the quality of worldwide education. Under the *Earth Constitution* and the Education Act of the Provisional World Parliament,
students will be encouraged to examine cultural
forms that suppress other human beings, for
example, through dress codes, pre-defined cultural roles or other such social practices. Such a
system cannot be entirely created *a priori* ahead
of time. What can be provided ahead of time is
a dynamic framework like the *Earth Constitution*
that allows creativity and innovation in struc-
turing a world peace system such as that shown
by the Provisional World Parliament.

Finally, these six elements in the world peace
system set up by the *Constitution* are comple-
mented and enlivened by the several other features specified in this conceptual model. If the
world is converted to a prosperity system, a justice system, a freedom system, and a sustainability system, then the grounds for war and
violence will have been substantially under-
cut. The *Constitution* creates a dynamic world
system that includes a multiplicity of agencies
and branches working together under common

holistic principles directed toward these goals. As one thinker put it: "A diverse system with multiple pathways and redundancies is more stable and less vulnerable to external shock than a uniform system with little diversity" (Meadows, 2008: 3-4). All these factors deriving from the holistic paradigm of unity in diversity at the heart of the *Constitution* work together to create a truly new historical era for human civilization. A stable, diverse world peace system derives from the holistic structure of the *Constitution* itself.

A Prosperity System—The New Democratic Economics

The present global economic system, like the system of sovereign nation-states, has evolved out of European civilization since the Renaissance, both systems slowly becoming the official doctrines concerning what is "natural" politically and economically. The so-called "natural" political organization of sovereign states was recognized at the Treaty of Westphalia in 1648, and the so-called "natural" system of economic laws was described in Adam Smith's *Wealth of Nations* that appeared in 1776. In both cases the imperial arrogance of Europe began the process of imposing these "natural" systems on the rest of humankind. For centuries we have seen the triumph of the nation-state system (described above) as a system of perpetual wars, violence, and chaos. Today, we also witness the triumph of the system of monopoly capitalism in the form of immense poverty, scarcity, and misery for at least 60% of the people on Earth simultaneously with unimaginable wealth and power for the mere 1% of the Earth's population who own 40% of its wealth.

Impartial observers have pointed out that this 1% uses the chaos of the present system of sovereign nations to further consolidate their wealth and power. Only by democratizing the world system can we change this horrific condition and create a prosperity system for the Earth. Authentic democracy cannot function when the few control such wealth and power. This cruel, irrational, and environmentally disastrous system can only be transformed when government functions on behalf of the universal rights and biospheric integrity of all the people of Earth and no longer on behalf of the ruling classes of some 193 autonomous nation-states.

The sovereign nation-state system integrated with monopoly capitalism leads to mayhem not only between countries but within countries. World Bank and IMF imposed economic "reforms" have led to economic disaster after disaster as "structural adjustment" destroys regional markets and opens countries up to predatory corporations and exploitative economic control from the imperial centers of capital. In *The Globalization of Poverty: Impacts of IMF and World Bank Reforms* (1999), economist Michel Chossudovsky chronicles the destruction of peoples worldwide under the onslaught of neocolonial greed run from the financial centers of capital.

In many cases (such as the infamous genocide in Rwanda) massive human rights violations were the direct consequence of the destruction of the economy by predatory control from abroad. Desperate people whose economies have disintegrated are likely to turn to irrational and murderous violence. Many other studies, such as Catherine Caufield's *Masters of Illusion: The World Bank and the Poverty of Nations* (1996) and Bruce Rich's *Mortgaging the Earth: The World Bank, Environmental Impoverishment, and the Crisis of Development* (1994) have shown similar results.

A main reason why the above mentioned series of events occurs and leads to breakdown of civil order and human rights violations is because the imperial centers of power define human rights in an entirely arbitrary and circumscribed manner. Human rights for them are limited to the traditional "political" rights. A poverty stricken society or government is supposed to respect freedom of speech and press, due process, voting procedures, etc. Starving people in the face of economic chaos caused by predatory economics from the imperial centers

or the World Bank are supposed to respect one
another's political rights. The consistent policy
of the U.S. has been to treat the U.N. Universal
Declaration of Human Rights (that includes economic and social rights) as "merely symbolic,"
having no authoritative force (Blum 2000).

A major cause of the violations of political
human rights today is because people worldwide are denied their economic and social
rights—the rights to a living wage, to healthcare, to social security, to adequate leisure time,
to educational opportunities, etc. As we have
seen, these are all features intrinsic to genuine
democracy. When people are economically exploited and destitute, it is pointless to speak to
them about respecting political rights. The *Earth
Constitution* transforms this situation through
the simple mechanism of presenting two bills of
rights, Articles 12 and 13. Article 13 guarantees
economic, social, and environmental rights to
every citizen of the Federation creating a world
where economic exploitation and chaos (due to
a denial of economic and social rights) do not
and cannot lead to a corresponding massive violation of political rights.

The other side of this coin of human rights
violations is the practice of imperial nations
in training the military elites of Third World
nations in what is euphemistically known as
"counterinsurgency warfare." The top secret
school at Fort Benning, Georgia, in the United

States (formerly known as the "School of the Americas") is only one example of this systematic foreign policy run from the imperial centers of the world. The militaries of Third World countries are trained in warfare against their own populations, in murder, blackmail, disappearances, torture, and other means of repression (cf. Hodge and Cooper 2004; Chomsky 1996: 29-34; Klein 2008). Human economic and political rights cannot be respected within the conceptual framework of war (whether this be a war on drugs, "rogue states," or terrorism), for war is precisely the barbarous no-holds-barred attempt to destroy a perceived "enemy."

The real job of these military and paramilitary juntas is to protect the *status quo* by maintaining a "stable investment climate" for multinational corporations and their backers of the global economic system of domination by the Pentagon and others. Protection of human rights is indeed "merely symbolic" under the system of sovereign nation-states, with its inherent domination of the weak by the strong and inherent system of global economic exploitation. Transforming the global paradigm to a non-military federation with an independent branch of government (the World Ombudsmus) serving to protect political, social, economic, and environmental rights worldwide will by and large solve the problem of human rights violations that has plagued the twentieth and twenty-first centuries (see Klein 2008).

Article 13 of the *Earth Constitution* guarantees equal opportunity for employment with wages sufficient for living with dignity, free and adequate public education for everyone, free and adequate public health services and medical care, protection of the natural environment, conservation of essential natural resources, adequate housing, nutritious food supplies, safe drinking water, and social security for all citizens to protect against accident and to assure dignity in old age. None of these elements in a universal prosperity system can be realized under the present global economic system based on private ownership of natural resources, especially land, and accumulation of wealth for the few at the expense of the many. Global prosperity can only be actualized through effective economic and political democracy on a planetary scale.

Under genuine global democracy there can be no more economic imperialism of corporations or nations, no more sweatshops, no more economic exploitation, nor more externalization of costs to the environment and the public by businesses, and no more interference with planetary democracy through manipulations by the rich. As with the world peace system, a world prosperity system will be institutionalized and maintained by the World Parliament, the World Executive, the World Courts, the World Police,

and the World Ombudsmus. The money supply will be public, and debt-free. Most production will be richly cooperative with the costs of
production, even when private, no longer exter-
nalized into the earth, air, and water. For the
first time in history, the *Earth Constitution* will
establish the reasonable economic and political
equality of all persons that are essential to effective democracy.

In short, the *Earth Constitution* creates a
democratic world commonwealth directed to
the common good of humanity and future
generations.   As we have seen, it is non-
military by law (Article 2) and democratic
at every level, leaving economic and political self-determination to the nations insofar as
these conform to universal human rights and
world law (Article 14). Hence, the three major non-democratic sources of the deep violence of today's world—sovereign nation-states,
transnational corporations, and global banking
cartels—are brought under the democratic control of the people of Earth through enforceable
world law.

Our global monetary system today is 99%
composed of privately created debt-money
(Brown 2007). Because of this we live in a
world of global scarcity and desperation requiring, as we have seen, massive military training for counterinsurgency warfare and massive
military interventions by imperial nations de-

signed to protect and promote the present world domination by a tiny corporate and financial elite. The *Earth Constitution* explicitly states that money must be created by the Federation as *debt-free money* addressed to the common good and planetary prosperity (Article 8.7.1.6 and 8.7.1.7).

Therefore, and perhaps most importantly, the Earth Federation issues debt-free, interest-free money to promote the prosperity, free trade, and well-being of the people of Earth while protecting the planetary environment. Individuals, corporations, state and local governments may all take advantage of very low cost development loans and lines of credit that are not premised on exploitation of the debtors in the service of private profit (Article 4). In addition, primary created (debt-free) money will be judiciously spent for global infrastructure needs by the World Parliament. Money and banking are now used in the service of the common good of the people of Earth and in protection of the "ecological fabric of life" on our planet. The rich can no longer exploit poor people and nations through a system of loans and debt that has so far created such misery for the peoples and nations of Earth.

Three key features of the corrupt oligarchy that now dominates the world economy are eliminated from the start. First, military Keynesianism (or militarism used to artificially pump up the economies of nations) is eliminated, since

under Article 2 all militaries worldwide become
illegal. The immense profitability and incentive for war based within the industrial-military
complex is abolished. Second, legal corporate
personhood is abolished. This legal decep-
tion has turned the once beneficial corporations
of the world into monstrous, immortal super-
humans, who use their billions of dollars and
super-human legal rights to dominate the economy of our planet. Third, the *Constitution* also
removes the ability of these corporate entities
and the super-rich to influence politics, judges,
and government officials through massive campaign contributions or other forms of monetary
influence.

Hence, the key steps necessary to founding
a truly democratic and prosperous world order take place with the ratification of the *Constitution*: the hold of the industrial-military oli-
garchies now dominating the planet is broken
along with the hold of their associates, the
banking, corporate, and massive financial oli-
garchies, and the monetary system of the world
is placed in the service of the people of Earth.
Achieving universal reasonable prosperity is
not difficult under these conditions. The founding of world democracy under the *Earth Constitution* accomplishes all this from its very incep-
tion.

These principles cannot work, we have seen,
unless we take the concept of "all" seriously

and universalize democracy to every person on
Earth. In the words of the U.N. Universal Declaration: "Every person has the right to life, liberty, and security of person." This universal-
ization process is the fundamental imperative
of our time. Yet there is a concomitant aspect
of our moral obligation today that requires us
to abjure violence, war, and military service altogether and create a world order premised on
substantive justice and fairness for all peoples.
As an integrated whole, the world peace system
and the world prosperity system created by the
Constitution will necessarily also be a world justice system.

A Justice System

Since the time of Aristotle, thinkers have distin-
guished two dimensions of justice: distributive
justice that considers how the resources of society can best be distributed, taking into consideration both the common good of society and
the principle that equal rewards should follow
equal accomplishments, and corrective justice in
which society sets up a system of trials, judg-
ments, and punishments for those who break
the laws (or to settle civil disputes). Historically the concept of justice has also been developed as the moral idea of fairness: the idea of
treating individuals or peoples fairly or equi-

tably. The *Earth Constitution* and the Provisional
World Parliament have extensively developed
all these aspects of justice.

The same integrated set of governmental
branches integral to the peace system and the
prosperity system work to operate the justice
system under the *Constitution*. With the help
of many departments gathering data on world
economic and social conditions, the World Parliament of some 1500 lawmakers representing
all peoples, nations, and the common good of
humanity studies the needs of the people of
Earth and makes laws directed toward peace,
universal prosperity, justice, freedom, and sustainability. All persons as individuals (including
all government officials) are held responsible to
these laws.

The World Police and Attorneys General
identify, indict, and apprehend suspects accused of violating world laws. We have seen
that the police have only such weapons that are
necessary to apprehend *individuals*. The requirement that police protect innocent bystanders is
also emphasized, as is the humane and digni-
fied treatment of those who are arrested and
held for a fair and impartial trial (Article 12.13
and 12.14). The professional and highly qualified world judiciary within the Earth Federation Civil Service framework conducts impartial trials of those accused, and the World Ombudsmus carefully watches to see that human

rights are protected throughout the process.

Under this system of correctional justice, no longer will the law and punishment be directed primarily toward the poor, with the overwhelming majority of those incarcerated coming from poor and disadvantaged background and subject to the kinds of laws and profiling that in effect punish the poor for being poor. Developing the spirit and intent of the *Constitution* with regard to correctional justice, the Provisional World Parliament has articulated the kinds of laws and corresponding punishments that will be fundamental to the justice system of the Earth Federation. It has worked out a system of seven classes of felonies, with corresponding punishments for conviction depending on the seriousness of the offense. (The World Penal Code is elaborated in detail in WLA # 19.) Those apprehended and tried under the Earth Federation will no longer be the poor but all persons who violate the laws regarding peace, general prosperity, justice, freedom, or sustainability.

The system of *distributive* justice under the *Earth Constitution* and Provisional World Parliament is equally transformative of the present disastrous world order. We have seen that Article 13 of the *Earth Constitution* guarantees equal opportunity for employment with wages sufficient to assure human dignity, free and adequate public education for everyone, free and adequate public health services and medical care, protection of the natural environment, conservation of essential natural resources, adequate housing, nutritious food supplies and safe drinking water, and social security for all citizens to protect against accident and assure dignity in old age. Distributive justice first and foremost recognizes universal human dignity and the right of every person to the livable income necessary to be free from extreme misery and deprivation.

The system of correctional justice will complement the system of distributive justice. The vast majority of people will see for themselves that things are truly fair and just in the moral sense. It should be clear that the justice system also requires the peace system and the prosperity system as we have described them. This equitable system of justice will also empower the freedom system which depends on, and derives from, a just world framework.

A Freedom System

Freedom, the protection of individual human rights premised on the autonomy and dignity of the individual person, is a multi-dimensional concept that lies at the very heart of democracy. We have seen the many ways in which the several branches of the Earth Federation government work together to ensure peace, prosperity, and justice. The same is true of freedom. The Earth Federation system as a whole ensures and undergirds freedom through dozens of features working together. It understands that freedom requires health, education, and sufficiency of resources. Extreme poverty is itself a denial of freedom. Political freedom must necessarily be complimented by economic and social freedom.

Article 12 of the *Earth Constitution* specifies 18 items articulating a series of political rights and freedoms. It even includes seven items that begin with the word "freedom"—"freedom of thought and conscience, speech, press, writing, etc.; freedom of assembly, association, etc.; freedom to vote and campaign; freedom of religion or no religion; freedom for political beliefs or no political beliefs; and freedom for investigation, research, and reporting. Article 13 also includes five items that begin with the words "free" or "freedom"—freedom of choice in work or profession; free public education and equal opportunities; free public health services and medical care; freedom of self-determination for dissenters or minorities; freedom for change of residence anywhere on Earth. The *Earth Constitution* addresses these multiple dimensions of human freedom (see Martin 2010b).

Article 12 calls all the rights that it specifies "inalienable" and states that "it shall be mandatory for the World Parliament, the World executive, and all organs and agencies of the World

Government to honor, implement, and enforce
these rights. All persons whose rights have been
violated "have full recourse through the World
Ombudsmus, the Enforcement System, and the
World Courts." Ultimately, however, freedom is
most fundamentally assured through the establishment of a *global community* under the *Earth
Constitution* dedicated to human development
and the actualization of human potential. No
longer will people be enslaved to multinational
corporations, banking cartels, or national security state domination. These impediments will
be brought into line by the global founded community of rights and responsibilities deriving
from legislation empowering individuals from
the ground up.

Aware that the greatest danger to freedom
historically has been government itself, especially the Executive Branch of government in
control of police and military, the framers of the
Constitution separated the police from the Executive branch, as we have seen, and abolished the
military altogether (beginning with the second
operative stage of the Earth Federation). The
Executive Branch of the Federation that admin-
isters the day to day operations of many government agencies is run by a presidium of five persons, one from each continental division of the
planet. The Executive has no power to declare
a state of emergency and suspend the *Constitution*, and it has no power to refuse to spend the

budget allocated to it by the World Parliament (Article 6.6).

The World Police and Attorneys General, we have seen, are a separate agency responsible directly to Parliament (representing the people of Earth). The police possess only weapons necessary to apprehend individuals and, like all government officials, can be removed for cause. The World Ombudsmus, is an independent agency of government responsible to the World Parliament that can investigate and indict the police for violations of human rights. The *Constitution* provides a comprehensive system of checks and balances directed toward protecting freedom and democracy.

Article 13 of the *Earth Constitution* presents an additional 19 items articulating a series of human rights that are often referred to as "second generation rights" and "third generation rights." The rights elaborated in Article 12 constitute the traditional political freedoms deriving from the 18th century democratic revolutions: freedom of speech, assembly, press, religion, etc. The conception of second generation rights developed through the early 20th century and were famously expressed, for example, in the U.N. Universal Declaration of Human Rights of 1948.

These include the rights to decent wages, healthcare, social security, education, etc. They are predicated on the understanding that a supportive *social framework* is a necessary foundation for personal freedom and dignity. These are elaborated in Article 13 of the *Earth Constitution*. However, the *Constitution* understands that even these are insufficient for true freedom. The positive fullness of freedom can only be realized on Earth when people are also guaranteed the "third generation" rights to world peace and protection of the global environment. The *Constitution* takes freedom to a higher level than any previous historical form.

We have seen that the founding principle of the *Earth Constitution* is unity in diversity, a principle that the Federation will promote throughout the government as well as in media, education, and law. The second "broad function" of the Earth Federation specified in Article 1 of the *Constitution* states that it must "protect universal human rights, including life, liberty, security, democracy, and equal opportunities in life." The entire system of the *Constitution* is built around this and the other five broad functions specified in Article 1, the first of which (Article 1.1) is world peace, the second of which (1.2) is freedom and the protection of human rights, and the fifth of which is "to protect the environment and the ecological fabric of life." The *Constitution* is specifically designed to enhance human flourishing and freedom throughout its many dimensions.

Major impediments to human freedom and

flourishing endemic to the present world disorder are removed and prevented from recurring by the integrated functions of the Earth Federation under the *Constitution*. For example, there will be no more national security state, world militarism, authoritarian regimes, rogue militarized terror groups, corporate violations of the dignity of employees, extremes of poverty and deprivation, lack of literacy and education, or lack of adequate health care. Scholars sometimes speak of the defense of first generation political rights as "negative freedom"—the removal of impediments to individual self-determination.

However, the *Constitution* will also enhance the "positive freedom" of actualization within an empowering community premised on unity in diversity. The supporting matrix of a community of rights and responsibilities premised as well on second and third generation rights provides the framework for the creative actualization of our individual and collective human potential. The protection of "life, security, and equal opportunities" on Earth, institutionalized through a global community of freedom (as specified in Article 1) will vastly empower the people of Earth. Freedom will no longer merely be a "freedom from" but will become the positive fullness of "freedom for." The *Earth Constitution* establishes a dynamic and powerful freedom system.

A Sustainability System

Environmental destruction (like war, poverty, injustice, and denial of freedom) is a direct consequence of our present global political and economic system. If companies have to consider the bottom line in a competitive situation where they must make a certain margin of profit or go out of business, then the incentive to *externalize* costs into the air, water, and soil to the detriment of the planetary ecosystem and future generations is tremendous. Genuine sustainability can only be achieved when the common good and the welfare of future generations are factored into the economic equation. Sustainability means that the resources taken from the Earth are either replaced fully (for example, lumber used in moderation can be replaced though replanting forests) or used sparingly until ways can be found to substitute artificial resources for essential natural resources (Daly 1996).

The *Earth Constitution* contains dozens of references to "the environment" and the "ecology" of our planet, indicating that a major premise of the Earth Federation will be environmental sustainability. The *Constitution* mundializes those natural resources that are vital to the well-being of humanity and that are limited in quantity or non-renewable (Article 4). Hence, they are taken out of the hands of giant corporate monopolies who today exploit them for the private profit of a few at the expense of most of humanity and future generations. The Provisional World Parliament has taken steps to enable this constitutional mandate, for example, by passing the Water Act at its Eight Session. Multinational corporations have bought up water rights in India and elsewhere and used their "right to private property" to blackmail ordinary citizens who need water (see Shiva 2002).

In his book *When Corporations Rule the World* (1995), former Harvard Business School professor, David Korten, chronicles the devastation of our natural resources as well as the environment by multinational corporations based in the imperial centers of capital. Natural resources are essential for human well-being and need to be carefully conserved for the well-being of all the Earth's citizens as well as future generations. The Provisional World Parliament created the World Oceans and Seabeds Authority to supervise the vast riches of the oceans for the welfare of humanity, oceans now being exploited by predatory nation-states and private corporations without any democratic governmental supervision.

With the vast power placed in human hands by engines, electricity, specialized machines, and computers, the ecosystems of the Earth began to be destroyed at a rate far beyond the ability of nature to heal and repair damages caused by human interference. The technological revolutions of the 18th and 19th centuries continued into the electronic and digital revolutions of the 20th and 21st centuries—placing such power in human hands that human activity in its present forms may well destroy the life-support systems of the entire planet and collapse the fabric of life to the point where higher forms of life can no longer survive upon the Earth. The forests of the world, for example, provide the planetary ecosystem with much of the oxygen that supports all aerobic forms of life. They bind carbon dioxide that is exhaled by most living creatures and produced by all forms of combustion. They moderate the climate and provide habitats for most of the vast bio-diversity of the Earth; they draw fresh water from the ocean coasts into the interior of continents. Yet the forests of the Earth are disappearing at the rate of an area one half the size of California each year.

In addition to forests, agricultural soils of the Earth are rapidly disappearing. Unsustainable agricultural practices are rapidly depleting topsoils of the planet to the point where vast areas have become unsuitable for agriculture and have been converted to grazing lands. Yet overgrazing worldwide is turning even these areas on every continent into desert wasteland, places that cannot be used to support most life. Runoff from the use of pesticides is poisoning water supplies and ecosystems. Billions of tons of topsoil are lost each year to erosion because of these unsustainable agricultural practices.

Regarding fresh water, the over-pumping of aquifers and overuse of water is dropping water tables worldwide, causing water crises and shortages in many areas of the world. The cities of the world, in addition, are becoming poisoners of the planet's fresh air supplies. Hundreds of millions of gasoline and internal combustion engines and other sources of air pollution spew pollutants into the air. Yet the atmosphere of the Earth is necessary to support all higher forms of life and is at the heart of the ecosystem of our planet.

These cities also produce immense amounts of polluted water, garbage, and trash wastes that are filling and poisoning countrysides, rivers, and oceans worldwide. At the same time, the human population continues to grow at the rate of some 80 million new persons per year, every person of whom requires basic resources, fresh water, clean air, and agricultural and forest resources to support them throughout their lifespans, and every one of whom produces waste materials that are returned to the environment (cf. Caldicott 1992; Renner 1996, Daly 1996; Speth 2004).

The principle of Gaia, the idea that the entire Earth (as it has evolved over its 4.6 billion year existence) forms an encompassing ecosystem, is only slowly becoming understood by large numbers of people. This awareness grows as planetary phenomena signaling the alteration of the entire global ecosystem become widely known. Phenomena such as global warming, melting of the polar ice caps, depletion of the ozone layer, collapsing of entire ocean fisheries, rapid extinction of species on a daily basis, increased planetary disasters and superstorms, and possible inversions of global ocean currents and weather patterns are well understood (Lovelock 1991).

Thoughtful human beings today have understood that human life is inseparable from the web of life on Earth. They have understood that we must alter our economic, social, and political practices rapidly to bring human civilization into harmony with the planetary web of life that sustains us. They understand that all development must be sustainable, that it must support human life in the present in ways that do not diminish the life-prospects of future generations. Today, virtually all societies and all nations are living at the expense of future generations, both of humans and other species (Caldicott 1992; Daly 1996; Speth 2004). Actualization of our life-prospects diminishes their life-prospects. At the current rate of destruction, it is even possible that we will reduce their life-prospects to zero.

The *Earth Constitution* and the work of the Provisional World Parliament have been dedicated to addressing these horrific consequences of the present world disorder. This premise of our global, democratically conceived, well-being is behind the Parliament's passage of the World Hydrogen Energy Authority (WLA #10) to spearhead research and conversion to renewable clean energy for the world, the Hydrocarbon Resource Act (WLA #16) to conserve, regulate on behalf of a clean environment, and utilize democratically the world's remaining hydrocarbon resources, and the Water Act (WLA #30) that recognizes clean water as a right of all persons and takes steps to protect the Earth's diminishing water resources, restore sources of fresh water to the Earth, and democratically apportion these resources to all persons on Earth.

Recognizing not only that the global environment is threatened but that it is already seriously damaged (as the *Manifesto of the Earth Federation* demonstrates at length), the Provisional World Parliament at its Second Session adopted WLA #6 creating the Emergency Earth Rescue Administration (EERA). The task of the EERA is to spearhead the gigantic task of restoring the environment of the Earth once the first operative stage of world government under the *Constitution* has been activated. Millions of trees will need to be planted, major initiatives will be needed to restore diminished agricultural lands, and emergency efforts will be required to reclaim sources and conditions for fresh water for the peoples of Earth.

The Parliament also passed WLA #9 creating,

within the World Administration of the *Constitution*, a Global Ministry of the Environment to facilitate conversion to sustainability and staff the EERA. Such momentous tasks, absolutely necessary for a decent future for the Earth, can never be accomplished by the fragmented system of nation-states or the U.N. The U.N., which is a mere confederation of sovereign nation-states, has held three global conferences on the destruction of our planetary environment: in Rio de Janeiro, Brazil, in 1992, Johannesburg, South Africa, in 2002, and Copenhagen, Denmark, in 2009. There is common agreement that these were all complete failures in dealing with our environmental crises.

The Provisional World Parliament has created a network of practical, pragmatic, and immediately necessary laws and agencies to deal with the immense problems of global environmental restoration and conversion to sustainability. As we have seen, the very first article of the *Earth Constitution* specifies that the fifth broad function of the Earth Federation will be "to protect the environment and the ecological fabric of life from all sources of damage, and to control technological innovations whose effects transcend national boundaries, for the purpose of keeping Earth a safe, healthy and happy home for humanity." Both the *Constitution* and the Parliament are dedicated to creating a world system adequate to this task.

The *Constitution* explicitly requires the government of the Earth Federation to protect the ecological fabric of life on Earth, that is, to respect the Gaia principle with all its ramifications. Not only does the *Constitution* make this a primary mandate of the Earth Federation, but in its second bill of rights (Article 13) makes respect for the Gaia principle a right of the people of Earth themselves and a "directive principle for the world government" to actualize this right. Article 13, numbers 9, 10, and 11 read as follows. People have a right to: "protection of the natural environment which is the common heritage of humanity against pollution, ecological disruption or damage which could imperil life or lower the quality of life" (9); "Conservation of those natural resources of Earth which are limited so that present and future generations may continue to enjoy life on planet Earth" (10); and "assurance for everyone of adequate housing, of adequate and nutritious food supplies, of safe and adequate water supplies, of pure air with protection of oxygen supplies and the ozone layer, and in general for the continuance of an environment which can sustain healthy living for all" (11).

Clearly, here again, the *Constitution* explicitly recognizes the need for human economic, political, and social institutions to conform to the Gaia principle (which is the principle of sustainability) protecting the whole of the planetary environment for future generations. The key to a sustainable civilization is not only to promote education concerning the principles of natural ecology. This effort alone is insufficient and will ultimately fail unless the anti-ecological institutions of the modern world, described above, are also transformed according to the scientific principles of natural ecology.

For this to happen, the entire human community must be joined together through the dynamic of genuine unity in diversity that constitutes a complementary principle of social ecology in human life, uniting all people under non-military democratic world government. Only thus can the Gaia principle become a guiding principle for all human political, economic, and social processes. These principles of social ecology are inseparable from the principles of natural ecology. It is necessary to do for humanity what the natural Gaia principle does for nature. The *Constitution for the Federation of Earth* joins the two together to create a truly ecological and sustainable world order.

Conclusion

The *Constitution* and its elaboration through the work of the Provisional World Parliament provide the necessary conditions for a peaceful, prosperous, and sustainable world system.

Throughout our model, however, we have assumed the creative input of the human beings with integrity, vision, and creative energy who must enliven the system outlined by the *Constitution* and the Parliament. The Earth Federation needs Parliamentarians, Judges, Administrators, Police, and Ombudsmen of who are capable of cooperatively working as part of an open ended, democratic learning community informed by the dynamics of systems thinking and the principles of holism. We need dedicated people who are willing to begin living from this moment forward according to the ethical and legal principles embodied in the *Earth Constitution*.

Such persons will serve as the sufficient condition for actualizing the unity in diversity of this world system. Such persons in our present historical situation must also serve as the sufficient condition for the ratification and implementation of the *Constitution*. The necessary features of a holistic world system can be described in print. The sufficient conditions for its actualization depend on the love, aspirations, conscience, and intelligence of actual human beings. Within the Earth Federation Movement today, citizens all around the world are actualizing this vision and have begun living according to the *Earth Constitution*, no longer according to the illegitimate and immoral system of warring nation-states.

The holism of the new, liberating paradigm discovered by 20th century science was embodied in the *Earth Constitution* by establishing social and economic systems designed to produce the holistic consequences of peace, prosperity, justice, freedom, and sustainability. It is this insight that is essential to human liberation. War and poverty are not essential to the human condition but are consequences of the global systems under which we currently struggle. If we establish different systems, different consequences will follow. You as a reader are engaging the most important document of the 20th century, which can form the bases for a new and liberating world system in the 21st century.

Study of the *Constitution for the Federation of Earth* repays the student richly. For a model of a future world order emerges that not only transforms the fragmented and outdated paradigms of the present world disorder but shows itself to be entirely practical and imminently possible under the guidelines provided by Articles 17 and 19. The conceptual model presented here and affirmed by the Provisional World Parliament at its 12th session in Kolkata, India, in 2010 presents only the highlights of the integrated planetary system initiated by the *Earth Constitution* and the Provisional World Parliament. I hope that the parameters of this model that I have sketched in this document may inspire people to evermore intensive study of the

Earth Constitution and modeling of the transformed world system that it engenders.

As people begin to understand the vision,
there is tremendous urgency that they also act
on that vision with creativity, integrity, and energy. The *Constitution* must be ratified in a
founding ratification convention according to
the Protocols already developed by the Provisional World Parliament. It converts the present
failed world system to peace, prosperity, justice,
freedom, and sustainability. It replaces the U.N.
Charter, with real democratic government keeping the valuable agencies of the U.N. as min-
istries of the Earth Federation. You are about to
read the most important document produced by
the 20th century—the document that will provide the foundation stone for the paradigm shift
of the 21st century. *Nothing less than the fate of
humanity and our precious planet Earth are at stake.
We invite your participation. We invite you to a life
of "civil obedience."*

Works Cited

Birch, Charles & Cobb, Jr., John B. (1990).*The Liberation
    of Life.* Denton, TX: Environmental Ethics Books.

Blum, William (2000). *Rogue State: A Guide to the
    World's Only Superpower.* Monroe, Maine: Com-
    mon Courage Press.

Brown, Ellen Hodgson (2007). *Web of Debt—The Shock-*

ing Truth about Our Money System. Baton Rouge, Louisiana: Third Millennium Press.

Caldicott, Helen (1992). *If You Love This Planet.* New York: W.W. Norton & Company.

Capra, Fritjof (1996). *The Web of Life: The New Scientific Understanding of Living Systems.* New York: Random House.

Caufield, Catherine (1996). *Masters of Illusion: The World Bank and the Poverty of Nations.* New York: Henry Holt & Company.

Chase-Dunn, Christopher (1998). *Global Formation: Structures of World Economy.* New York: Rowman & Littlefield.

Chomsky, Noam (1996). *What Uncle Sam Really Wants.* Berkeley: Odonian Press.

Chossudovsky, Michel (1999). *The Globalization of Poverty: Impacts of IMF and World Bank Reforms.* London: Zed Books, LTD.

Daly, Herman E. (1996). *Beyond Growth: The Economics of Sustainable Development.* Boston: Beacon Press.

Fromm, Erich (1962). *Beyond the Chains of Illusion: My Encounter With Marx and Freud.* New York: Simon & Schuster.

Hegel, G.W.F. (1991). *Elements of the Philosophy of Right.* Alan Wood, ed. Cambridge: Cambridge University Press.

Hodge, James and Cooper, Linda (2004). *Disturbing the Peace: The Story of Father Roy Bourgeois and the Movement to Close the School of the Americas.*

Maryknoll, New York: Orbis Books.

Jacobson, Nolan Pliny (1982).   "A Buddhistic-Christian Probe of our Endangered Future." *The Eastern Buddhist.* Vol. XV, No. 1, Spring 1982.

Kant, Immanuel (1983). *Perpetual Peace and Other Essays.* Ted Humphrey, trans. Indianapolis: Hackett Publishing Company.

Klein, Naomi (2008). *The Shock Doctrine: the Rise of Disaster Capitalism.* New York: Henry Holt & Company.

Korten, David (1995).   *When Corporations Rule the World.* Second Edition. Bloomfield, CT: Kumarian Press.

Lovelock, James (1991).   *Healing Gaia: Practical Medicine for the Planet.* New York: Harmony Books.

Martin, Glen T. (2009). *Ascent to Freedom: Practical and Philosophical Foundations of Democratic World Law.* Pamplin, VA: Institute for Economic Democracy Press.

—(2010a).   *Constitution for the Federation of Earth: With Historical Introduction, Commentary, and Conclusion.*   Pamplin, VA: Institute for Economic Democracy Press.

—(2010b). *Triumph of Civilization: Democracy, Nonviolence, and the Piloting of Spaceship Earth.* Pamplin, VA: Institute for Economic Democracy Press.

—(2011). *The Earth Federation Movement: History, Documents, Philosophical Foundations.* Pamplin, VA: Institute for Economic Democracy Press.

Meadows, Donella H. (2008). *Thinking in Systems: A Primer*. White River Junction, VT: Chelsea Green Publishing Company.

Munitz, Milton K. (1986). *Cosmic Understanding: Philosophy and the Science of the Universe*. Princeton: Princeton University Press.

Renner, Michael (1996). *Struggling for Survival: Environmental Decline, Social Conflict, and the New Age of Insecurity*. New York: W. W. Norton & Co.

Rich, Bruce (1994). *Mortgaging the Earth: The World Bank, Environmental Impoverishment, and the Crisis of Development*. Boston: Beacon Press.

Shiva, Vandana (2002). *Water Wars: Privatization, Pollution, and Profit*. Boston: South End Press.

Speth, James Gustave (2004). *Red Sky at Morning: America and the Crisis of the Global Environment*. New Haven: Yale University Press.

Stapp, Henry (1988). In Kitchener, Richard F., ed. *The World View of Contemporary Physics: Does it Need a New Metaphysics?* Albany: State University of New York Press.

Williams, Chris (2010). *Ecology and Socialism: Solutions to Capitalist Ecological Crisis*. Chicago: Haymarket Books.

The Constitution for the Federation of the Earth

Preamble

Realizing that Humanity today has come to a turning point in history and that we are on the threshold of a new world order which promises to usher in an era of peace, prosperity, justice and harmony;

Aware of the interdependence of people, nations and all life;

Aware that man's abuse of science and technology has brought Humanity to the brink of disaster through the production of horrendous weaponry of mass destruction and to the brink of ecological and social catastrophe;

Aware that the traditional concept of security through military defense is a total illusion both for the present and for the future;

Aware of the misery and conflicts caused by
ever increasing disparity between rich and poor;

Conscious of our obligation to posterity to save
Humanity from imminent and total annihilation;

Conscious that Humanity is One despite the existence of diverse nations, races, creeds, ideologies and cultures and that the principle of
unity in diversity is the basis for a new age
when war shall be outlawed and peace prevail;
when the earth's total resources shall be equitably used for human welfare; and when basic human rights and responsibilities shall be
shared by all without discrimination;

Conscious of the inescapable reality that the
greatest hope for the survival of life on earth
is the establishment of a democratic world government;

We, citizens of the world, hereby resolve to establish a world federation to be governed in accordance with this Constitution for the Federation of Earth.

Article 1

Broad Functions of the Earth Federation

The broad functions of the Federation of Earth shall be:

1.1 To prevent war, secure disarmament, and resolve territorial and other disputes which endanger peace and human rights.

1.2 To protect universal human rights, including life, liberty, security, democracy, and equal opportunities in life.

1.3 To obtain for all people on earth the conditions required for equitable economic and social development and for diminishing social differences.

71

1.4 To regulate world trade, communications, transportation, currency, standards, use of world resources, and other global and international processes.

1.5 To protect the environment and the ecological fabric of life from all sources of damage, and to control technological innovations whose effects transcend national boundaries, for the purpose of keeping Earth a safe, healthy and happy home for humanity.

1.6 To devise and implement solutions to all problems which are beyond the capacity of national governments, or which are now or may become of global or international concern or consequence.

Article 2

Basic Structure of the Earth Federation

2.1 The Federation of Earth shall be organized as a universal federation, to include all nations and all people, and to encompass all oceans, seas and lands of Earth, inclusive of non-self governing territories, together with the surrounding atmosphere.

2.2 The World Government for the Federation of Earth shall be non-military and shall be democratic in its own structure, with ultimate sovereignty residing in all the people who live on Earth.

2.3 The authority and powers granted to the World Government shall be limited to those defined in this Constitution for the Federation of Earth, applicable to problems and affairs which transcend national boundaries, leaving to national governments jurisdiction over the internal affairs of the respective nations but consistent with the authority of the World Government to protect universal human rights as defined in this World Constitution.

2.4 The basic direct electoral and administrative units of the World Government shall be World Electoral and Administrative Districts. A total of not more than 1000 World Electoral and Administrative Districts shall be defined, and shall be nearly equal in population, within the limits of plus or minus ten percent.

2.5 Contiguous World Electoral and Administrative Districts shall be combined as may be appropriate to compose a total of twenty World Electoral and Administrative Regions for the following purposes, but not limited thereto: for the election or appointment of certain world government officials; for administrative purposes; for composing various organs of the world government as enumerated in Article 4; for the functioning of the Judiciary, the Enforcement System, and the Ombudsmus, as well as for the functioning of any other organ or agency of the World Government.

2.6 The World Electoral and Administrative Regions may be composed of a variable number of World Electoral and Administrative Districts, taking into consideration geographic, cultural, ecological and other factors as well as population.

2.7 Contiguous World Electoral and Administrative Regions shall be grouped together in pairs to compose Magna-Regions.

2.8 The boundaries for World Electoral and Administrative Regions shall not cross the boundaries of the World Electoral and Administrative Districts, and shall be common insofar as feasible for the various administrative departments and for the several organs and agencies of the World Government. Boundaries for the World Electoral and Administrative Districts as well as for the Regions need not conform to existing national boundaries, but shall conform as far as practicable.

2.9 The World Electoral and Administrative Regions shall be grouped to compose at least five Continental Divisions of the Earth, for the election or appointment of certain world government officials, and for certain aspects of the composition and functioning of the several organs and agencies of the World Government as specified hereinafter. The boundaries of Continental Divisions shall not cross existing national boundaries as far as practicable. Continental Divisions may be composed of a variable number of World Electoral and Administrative Regions.

Article 3

Organs of the Earth Federation

The organs of the World Government shall be:

3.1 The World Parliament

3.2 The World Executive

3.3 The World Administration

3.4 The Integrative Complex

3.5 The World Judiciary

3.6 The Enforcement System

3.7 The World Ombudsmus

Article 4

Grant of Specific Powers to the Earth Federation

The powers of the World government to be exercised through its several organs and agencies shall comprise the following:

4.1 Prevent wars and armed conflicts among the nations, regions, districts, parts and peoples of Earth.

4.2 Supervise disarmament and prevent rearmament; prohibit and eliminate the design, testing, manufacture, sale, purchase, use and possession of weapons of mass destruction, and prohibit or regulate all lethal weapons which the World Parliament may decide.

4.3 Prohibit incitement to war, and discrimination against or defamation of conscientious objectors.

4.4 Provide the means for peaceful and just solutions of disputes and conflicts among or between nations, peoples, and/or other components within the Federation of Earth.

4.5 Supervise boundary settlements and conduct plebiscites as needed.

4.6 Define the boundaries for the districts, regions and divisions which are established for electoral, administrative, judicial and other purposes of the World Government.

4.7 Define and regulate procedures for the nomination and election of the members of each House of the World Parliament, and for the nomination, election, appointment and employment of all World Government officials and personnel.

4.8 Codify world laws, including the body of international law developed prior to adoption of the world constitution, but not inconsistent therewith, and which is approved by the World Parliament.

4.9 Establish universal standards for weights, measurements, accounting and records.

4.10 Provide assistance in the event of large scale calamities, including drought, famine, pestilence, flood, earthquake, hurricane, ecological disruptions and other disasters.

4.11 Guarantee and enforce the civil liberties and the basic human rights which are defined in the Bill of Rights for the Citizens of Earth which is made a part of this World Constitution under Article 12.

4.12 Define standards and promote the worldwide improvement in working conditions, nutrition, health, housing, human settlements, environmental conditions, education, economic security, and other conditions defined under Article 13 of this World Constitution.

4.13 Regulate and supervise international transportation, communications, postal services, and migrations of people.

4.14 Regulate and supervise supra-national trade, industry, corporations, businesses, cartels, professional services, labor supply, finances, investments and insurance.

4.15 Secure and supervise the elimination of tariffs and other trade barriers among nations, but with provisions to prevent or minimize hardship for those previously protected by tariffs.

4.16 Raise the revenues and funds, by direct and/or indirect means, which are necessary for the purposes and activities of the World Government.

4.17 Establish and operate world financial, banking, credit and insurance institutions designed to serve human needs; establish, issue and regulate world currency, credit and exchange.

4.18 Plan for and regulate the development, use, conservation and recycling of the natural resources of Earth as the common heritage of Humanity; protect the environment in every way for the benefit of both present and future generations.

4.19 Create and operate a World Economic Development Organization to serve equitably the needs of all nations and people included within the World Federation.

4.20 Develop and implement solutions to transnational problems of food supply, agricultural production, soil fertility, soil conservation, pest control, diet, nutrition, drugs and poisons, and the disposal of toxic wastes.

4.21 Develop and implement means to control population growth in relation to the life-support capacities of Earth, and solve problems of population distribution.

4.22 Develop, protect, regulate and conserve the water supplies of Earth; develop, operate and/or coordinate transnational irrigation and other water supply and control projects; assure equitable allocation of trans-national water supplies, and protect against adverse trans-national effects of water or moisture diversion or weather control projects within national boundaries.

4.23 Own, administer and supervise the development and conservation of the oceans and sea-beds of Earth and all resources thereof, and protect from damage.

4.24 Protect from damage, and control and supervise the uses of the atmosphere of Earth.

4.25 Conduct inter-planetary and cosmic explorations and research; have exclusive jurisdiction over the Moon and over all satellites launched from Earth.

4.26 Establish, operate and/or coordinate global air lines, ocean transport systems, international railways and highways, global communication systems, and means for interplanetary travel and communications; control and administer vital waterways.

4.27 Develop, operate and/or coordinate transnational power systems, or networks of small units, integrating into the systems or networks power derived from the sun, wind, water, tides, heat differentials, magnetic forces, and any other source of safe, ecologically sound and continuing energy supply.

4.28 Control the mining, production, transportation and use of fossil sources of energy to the extent necessary to reduce and prevent damages to the environment and the ecology, as well as to prevent conflicts and conserve supplies for sustained use by succeeding generations.

4.29 Exercise exclusive jurisdiction and control over nuclear energy research and testing and nuclear power production, including the right to prohibit any form of testing or production considered hazardous.

4.30 Place under world controls essential natural resources which may be limited or unevenly distributed about the Earth. Find and implement ways to reduce wastes and find ways to minimize disparities when development or production is insufficient to supply everybody with all that may be needed.

4.31 Provide for the examination and assessment of technological innovations which are or may be of supranational consequence, to determine possible hazards or perils to humanity or the environment; institute such controls and regulations of technology as may be found necessary to prevent or correct widespread hazards or perils to human health and welfare.

4.32 Carry out intensive programs to develop safe alternatives to any technology or technological processes which may be hazardous to the environment, the ecological system, or human health and welfare.

4.33 Resolve supra-national problems caused by gross disparities in technological development or capability, capital formation, availability of natural resources, educational opportunity, economic opportunity, and wage and price differentials. Assist the processes of technology transfer under conditions which safeguard human

welfare and the environment and con-
tribute to minimizing disparities.

4.34 Intervene under procedures to be defined
by the World Parliament in cases of either
intra-state violence and intra-state problems which seriously affect world peace or
universal human rights.

4.35 Develop a world university system. Obtain the correction of prejudicialcommu-
nicative materials which cause misunder-
standings or conflicts due to differences of
race, religion, sex, national origin or affiliation.

4.36 Organize, coordinate and/or administer
a voluntary, non-military World Service
Corps, to carry out a wide variety of
projects designed to serve human welfare.

4.37 Designate as may be found desirable an
official world language or official world
languages.

4.38 Establish and operate a system of world
parks, wild life preserves, natural places,
and wilderness areas.

4.39 Define and establish procedures for initiative and referendum by the Citizens of
Earth on matters of supra-national legislation not prohibited by this World Constitution.

4.40 Establish such departments, bureaus, commissions, institutes, corporations, administrations, or agencies as may by needed to carry out any and all of the functions and powers of the World Government.

4.41 Serve the needs of humanity in any and all ways which are now, or may prove in the future to be, beyond the capacity of national and local governments.

Article 5

The World Parliament

Section 5.1 Functions and Powers of the World Parliament

5.1.1 To prepare and enact detailed legislation in all areas of authority and jurisdiction granted to the World Government under Article 4 of this World Constitution.

5.1.2 To amend or repeal world laws as may be found necessary or desirable.

5.1.3 To approve, amend or reject the international laws developed prior to the advent of World Government, and to codify and integrate the system of world law and world legislation under the World Government.

5.1.4 To establish such regulations and directions as may be needed, consistent with this world constitution, for the proper functioning of all organs, branches, departments, bureaus, commissions, institutes, agencies or parts of the World Government.

5.1.5 To review, amend and give final approval to each budget for the World Government, as submitted by the World Executive; to devise the specific means for directly raising funds needed to fulfill the budget, including taxes, licenses, fees, globally accounted social and public costs which must be added into the prices for goods and services, loans and credit advances, and any other appropriate means; and to appropriate and allocate funds for all operations and functions of the World Government in accordance with approved budgets, but subject to the right of the Parliament to revise any appropriation not yet spent or contractually committed.

5.1.6 To create, alter, abolish or consolidate the departments, bureaus, commissions, institutes, agencies or other parts of the World Government as may be needed for the best functioning of the several organs of the World Government, subject to the specific provisions of this World Constitution.

5.1.7 To approve the appointments of the heads of all major departments, commissions, offices, agencies and other parts of the several organs of the World Government, except those chosen by electoral or civil service procedures.

5.1.8 To remove from office for cause any member of the World Executive, and any elective or appointive head of any organ, department, office, agency or other part of the World Government, subject to the specific provisions in this World Constitution concerning specific offices.

5.1.9 To define and revise the boundaries of the World Electoral and Administrative Districts, the World Electoral and Administrative Regions and Magna Regions, and the Continental Divisions.

5.1.10 To schedule the implementation of those provisions of the World Constitution which require implementation by stages during the several stages of Provisional World Government, First Operative Stage of World Government, Second Operative Stage of World Government, and Full Operative Stage of World Government, as defined in Articles 17 and 19 of this World Constitution.

5.1.11 To plan and schedule the implementation of those provisions of the World Constitution which may require a period of years to be accomplished.

Section 5.2   Composition of the World Parliament

5.2.1 The World Parliament shall be composed of three houses, designated as follows:

- **The House of Peoples**, to represent the people of Earth directly and equally;
- **The House of Nations**, to represent the nations which are joined together in the Federation of Earth;
- **The House of Counsellors**, with particular functions to represent the highest good and best interests of humanity as a whole.

5.2.2 All members of the World Parliament, regardless of House, shall be designated as Members of the World Parliament.

Section 5.3   The House of Peoples

5.3.1 The House of Peoples shall be composed of the peoples delegates directly elected in proportion to population from the World Electoral and Administrative Districts, as defined in Article 2.4.

5.3.2 Peoples delegates shall be elected by universal adult suffrage, open to all persons of age 18 and above.

5.3.3 One peoples delegate shall be elected from each World Electoral and Administrative District to serve a five year term in the House of Peoples. Peoples delegates may be elected to serve successive terms without limit.   Each peoples delegate shall have one vote.

5.3.4 A candidate for election to serve as a peoples delegate must be at least 21 years of age, a resident for at least one year of the electoral district from which the candidate is seeking election, and shall take a pledge of service to humanity.

Section 5.4   The House of Nations

5.4.1 The House of Nations shall be composed of national delegates elected or appointed by procedures to be determined by each national government on the following basis:

5.4.1.1 One national delegate from each nation of at least 100,000 population, but less than 10,000,000 population.

5.4.1.2 Two national delegates from each nation of at least 10,000,000 population, but less than 100,000,000 population.

5.4.1.3 Three national delegates from each nation of 100,000,000 population or more.

5.4.2 Nations of less than 100,000 population may join in groups with other nations for purposes of representation in the House of Nations.

5.4.3 National delegates shall be elected or appointed to serve for terms of five years, and may be elected or appointed to serve successive terms without limit. Each national delegate shall have one vote.

5.4.4 Any person to serve as a national delegate shall be a citizen for at least two years of the nation to be represented, must be at least 21 years of age, and shall take a pledge of service to humanity.

Section 5.5   The House of Counsellors

5.5.1 The House of Counsellors shall be composed of 200 counsellors chosen in equal numbers from nominations submitted from the twenty World Electoral and Administrative Regions, as defined in Article 2.5. and 2.6., ten from each Region.

5.5.2 Nominations for members of the House of Counsellors shall be made by the teachers and students of universities and colleges and of scientific academies and institutes within each world electoral and administrative region. Nominees may be persons who are off campus in any walk of life as well as on campus.

5.5.3 Nominees to the House of Counsellors from each World Electoral and Administrative Region shall, by vote taken among themselves, reduce the number of nominees to no less than two times and no more than three times the number to be elected.

5.5.4 Nominees to serve as members of the House of Counsellors must be at least 25 years of age, and shall take a pledge of service to humanity. There shall be no residence requirement, and a nominee need not be a resident of the region from which nominated or elected.

5.5.5 The members of the House of Counsellors from each region shall be elected by the members of the other two houses of the World Parliament from the particular region.

5.5.6 Counsellors shall be elected to serve terms of ten years. One-half of the members of the House of Counsellors shall be elected every five years. Counsellors may serve successive terms without limit. Each Counsellor shall have one vote.

Section 5.6   Procedures of the World Parliament

5.6.1 Each house of the World Parliament during its first session after general elections shall elect a panel of five chairpersons from among its own members, one from each of five Continental Divisions. The chairpersons shall rotate annually so that each will serve for one year as chief presiding officer, while the other four serve as vice-chairpersons.

5.6.2 The panels of Chairpersons from each House shall meet together, as needed, for the purpose of coordinating the work of the Houses of the World Parliament, both severally and jointly.

5.6.3 Any legislative measure or action may be initiated in either House of Peoples or House of Nations or both concurrently, and shall become effective when passed by a simple majority vote of both the House of Peoples and of the House of Nations, except in those cases where an absolute majority vote or other voting majority is specified in this World Constitution.

5.6.4 In case of deadlock on a measure initiated in either the House of Peoples or House of Nations, the measure shall then automatically go to the House of Counsellors for decision by simple majority vote of the House of Counsellors, except in the cases where other majority vote is required in this World Constitution. Any measure may be referred for decision to the House of Counsellors by a concurrent vote of the other two houses.

5.6.5 The House of Counsellors may initiate any legislative measure, which shall then be submitted to the other two houses and must be passed by simple majority vote of both the House of Peoples and House of Nations to become effective, unless other voting majority is required by some provision of this World Constitution.

5.6.6 The House of Counsellors may introduce an opinion or resolution on any measure pending before either of the other two houses; either of the other houses may request the opinion of the House of Counsellors before acting upon a measure.

5.6.7 Each house of the World Parliament shall adopt its own detailed rules of procedure, which shall by consistent with the procedures set forth in this World Constitution, and which shall be designed to facilitate coordinated functioning of the three houses.

5.6.8 Approval of appointments by the World Parliament or any house thereof shall require simple majority votes, while removals for cause shall require absolute majority votes.

5.6.9 After the full operative stage of World Government is declared, general elections for members of the World Parliament to the House of Peoples shall be held every five years. The first general elections shall be held within the first two years following the declaration of the full operative stage of World Government.

5.6.10 Until the full operative stage of World Government is declared, elections for members of the World Parliament to the House of Peoples may be conducted whenever feasible in relation to the campaign for ratification of this World Constitution.

5.6.11 Regular sessions of the House of Peoples and House of Nations of the World Parliament shall convene on the second Monday of January of each and every year.

5.6.12 Each nation, according to its own procedures, shall appoint or elect members of the World Parliament to the House of Nations at least thirty days prior to the date for convening the World Parliament in January.

5.6.13 The House of Peoples together with the House of Nations shall elect the members of the World Parliament to the House of Counsellors during the month of January after the general elections. For its first session after general elections, the House of Counsellors shall convene on the second Monday of March, and thereafter concurrently with the other two houses.

5.6.14 Bi-elections to fill vacancies shall be held within three months from occurrence of the vacancy or vacancies.

5.6.15 The World Parliament shall remain in session for a minimum of nine months of each year. One or two breaks may be taken during each year, at times and for durations to be decided by simple majority vote of the House of Peoples and House of Nations sitting jointly.

5.6.16 Annual salaries for members of the World Parliament of all three houses shall be the same, except for those who serve also as members of the Presidium and of the Executive Cabinet.

5.6.17 Salary schedules for members of the World Parliament and for members of the Presidium and of the Executive Cabinet shall be determined by the World Parliament.

Article 6

The World Executive

Section 6.1   Functions and Powers of the World Executive

6.1.1 To implement the basic system of world law as defined in the World Constitution and in the codified system of world law after approval by the World Parliament.

6.1.2 To implement legislation enacted by the World Parliament.

6.1.3 To propose and recommend legislation for enactment by the World Parliament.

6.1.4 To convene the World Parliament in special sessions when necessary.

6.1.5 To supervise the World Administration and the Integrative Complex and all of the departments, bureaus, offices, institutes and agencies thereof.

6.1.6 To nominate, select and remove the heads of various organs, branches, departments, bureaus, offices, commissions, institutes, agencies and other parts of the World Government, in accordance with the provisions of this World Constitution and as specified in measures enacted by the World Parliament.

6.1.7 To prepare and submit annually to the World Parliament a comprehensive budget for the operations of the World Government, and to prepare and submit periodically budget projections over periods of several years.

6.1.8 To define and propose priorities for world legislation and budgetary allocations.

6.1.9 To be held accountable to the World Parliament for the expenditures of appropriations made by the World Parliament in accordance with approved and longer term budgets, subject to revisions approved by the World Parliament.

Section 6.2   Composition of the World Executive

The World Executive shall consist of a Presidium of five members, and of an Executive Cabinet of from twenty to thirty members, all of whom shall be members of the World Parliament.

Section 6.3   The Presidium

6.3.1 The Presidium shall be composed of five members, one to be designated as President and the other four to be designated as Vice Presidents. Each member of the Presidium shall be from a different Continental Division.

6.3.2 The Presidency of the Presidium shall rotate each year, with each member in turn to serve as President, while the other four serve as Vice Presidents. The order of rotation shall be decided by the Presidium.

6.3.3 The decisions of the Presidium shall be taken collectively, on the basis of majority decisions.

6.3.4 Each member of the Presidium shall be a member of the World Parliament, either elected to the House of Peoples or to the House of Counsellors, or appointed or elected to the House of Nations.

6.3.5 Nominations for the Presidium shall be made by the House of Counsellors. The number of nominees shall be from two to three times the number to be elected. No more than one-third of the nominees shall be from the House of Counsellors or from the House of Nations, and nominees must be included from all Continental Divisions.

6.3.6 From among the nominees submitted by the House of Counsellors, the Presidium shall be elected by vote of the combined membership of all three houses of the World Parliament in joint session. A plurality vote equal to at least 40 percent of the total membership of the World Parliament shall be required for the election of each member to the Presidium, with successive elimination votes taken as necessary until the required plurality is achieved.

6.3.7 Members of the Presidium may be removed for cause, either individually or collectively, by an absolute majority vote of the combined membership of the three houses of the World Parliament in joint session.

6.3.8 The term of office for the Presidium shall be five years and shall run concurrently with the terms of office for the members as Members of the World Parliament, except that at the end of each five year period, the Presidium members in office shall continue to serve until the new Presidium for the succeeding term is elected. Membership in the Presidium shall be limited to two consecutive terms.

Section 6.4   The Executive Cabinet

6.4.1 The Executive Cabinet shall be composed of from twenty to thirty members, with at least one member from each of the ten World Electoral and Administrative Magna Regions of the world.

6.4.2 All members of the Executive Cabinet shall be Members of the World Parliament.

6.4.3 There shall be no more than two members of the Executive Cabinet from any single nation of the World Federation. There may be only one member of the Executive Cabinet from a nation from which a Member of the World Parliament is serving as a member of the Presidium.

6.4.4 Each member of the Executive Cabinet shall serve as the head of a department or agency of the World Administration or Integrative Complex, and in this capacity shall be designated as Minister of the particular department or agency.

6.4.5 Nominations for members of the Executive Cabinet shall be made by the Presidium, taking into consideration the various functions which Executive Cabinets members are to perform. The Presidium shall nominate no more than two times the number to be elected.

6.4.6 The Executive Cabinet shall be elected by simple majority vote of the combined membership of all three houses of the World Parliament in joint session.

6.4.7 Members of the Executive Cabinet either individually or collectively may be removed for cause by an absolute majority vote of the combined membership of all three houses of the World Parliament sitting in joint session.

6.4.8 The term of office in the Executive Cabinet shall be five years, and shall run concurrently with the terms of office for the members as Members of the World Parliament, except that at the end of each five year period, the Cabinet members in office shall continue to serve until the new Executive Cabinet for the succeeding term is elected. Membership in the Executive Cabinet shall be limited to three consecutive terms, regardless of change in ministerial position.

Section 6.5   Procedures of the World Executive

6.5.1 The Presidium shall assign the ministerial positions among the Cabinet members to head the several administrative departments and major agencies of the Administration and of the Integrative Complex. Each Vice President may also serve as a Minister to head an administrative department, but not the President. Ministerial positions may be changed at the discretion of the Presidium. A Cabinet member or Vice President may hold more than one ministerial post, but no more than three, providing that no Cabinet member is without a Ministerial post.

6.5.2 The Presidium, in consultation with the Executive Cabinet, shall prepare and present to the World Parliament near the beginning of each year a proposed program of world legislation. The Presidium may propose other legislation during the year.

6.5.3 The Presidium, in consultation with the Executive Cabinet, and in consultation with the World Financial Administration, (see Article 8, Sec. 7.1.9.) shall be responsible for preparing and submitting to the World Parliament the proposed annual budget, and budgetary projections over periods of years.

6.5.4 Each Cabinet Member and Vice President as Minister of a particular department or agency shall prepare an annual report for the particular department or agency, to be submitted both to the Presidium and to the World Parliament.

6.5.5 The members of the Presidium and of the Executive Cabinet at all times shall be responsible both individually and collectively to the World Parliament.

6.5.6 Vacancies occurring at any time in the World Executive shall be filled within sixty days by nomination and election in the same manner as specified for filling the offices originally.

Section 6.6   Limitations on the World Executive

6.6.1 The World Executive shall not at any time alter, suspend, abridge, infringe or otherwise violate any provision of this World Constitution or any legislation or world law enacted or approved by the World Parliament in accordance with the provisions of this World Constitution.

6.6.2 The World Executive shall not have veto power over any legislation passed by the World Parliament.

6.6.3 The World Executive may not dissolve the World Parliament or any House of the World Parliament.

6.6.4 The World Executive may not act contrary to decisions of the World Courts.

6.6.5 The World Executive shall be bound to faithfully execute all legislation passed by the World Parliament in accordance with the provisions of this World Constitution, and may not impound or refuse to spend funds appropriated by the World Parliament, nor spend more funds than are appropriated by the World Parliament.

6.6.6 The World Executive may not transcend or contradict the decisions or controls of the World Parliament, the World Judiciary or the Provisions of this World Constitution by any device of executive order or executive privilege or emergency declaration or decree.

Article 7

The World Administration

Section 7.1   Functions of the World Administration

7.1.1 The World Administration shall be organized to carry out the detailed and continuous administration and implementation of world legislation and world law.

7.1.2 The World Administration shall be under the direction of the World Executive, and shall at all times be responsible to the World Executive.

7.1.3 The World Administration shall be organized so as to give professional continuity to the work of administration and implementation.

Section 7.2 Structure and Procedures of the World Administration

7.2.1 The World Administration shall be composed of professionally organized departments and other agencies in all areas of activity requiring continuity of administration and implementation by the World Government.

7.2.2 Each Department or major agency of the World Administration shall be headed by a Minister who shall be either a member of the Executive Cabinet or a Vice President of the Presidium.

7.2.3 Each Department or major agency of the World Administration shall have as chief of staff a Senior Administrator, who shall assist the Minister and supervise the detailed work of the Department or agency.

7.2.4 Each Senior Administrator shall be nominated by the Minister of the particular Department or agency from among persons in the senior lists of the World

Civil Service Administration, as soon as senior lists have been established by the World Civil Service Administration, and shall be confirmed by the Presidium. Temporary qualified appointments shall be made by the Ministers, with confirmation by the Presidium, pending establishment of the senior lists.

7.2.5 There shall be a Secretary General of the World Administration, who shall be nominated by the Presidium and confirmed by absolute majority vote of the entire Executive Cabinet.

7.2.6 The functions and responsibilities of the Secretary General of the World Administration shall be to assist in coordinating the work of the Senior Administrators of the several Departments and agencies of the World Administration. The Secretary General shall at all times be subject to the direction of the Presidium, and shall be directly responsible to the Presidium.

7.2.7 The employment of any Senior Administrator and of the Secretary General may be terminated for cause by absolute majority vote of both the Executive Cabinet and Presidium combined, but not contrary to civil service rules which protect tenure on grounds of competence.

7.2.8 Each Minister of a Department or agency of the World Administration, being also a Member of the World Parliament, shall provide continuous liaison between the particular Department or agency and the World Parliament, shall respond at any time to any questions or requests for information from the Parliament, including committees of any House of the World Parliament.

7.2.9 The Presidium, in cooperation with the particular Ministers in each case, shall be responsible for the original organization of each of the Departments and major agencies of the World Administration.

7.2.10 The assignment of legislative measures, constitutional provisions and areas of world law to particular Departments and agencies for administration and implementation shall be done by the Presidium in consultation with the Executive Cabinet and Secretary General, unless specifically provided in legislation passed by the World Parliament.

7.2.11 The Presidium, in consultation with the Executive Cabinet, may propose the creation of other departments and agencies to have ministerial status; and may propose the alteration, combination or termination of existing Departments and agencies of ministerial status as may seem necessary or desirable. Any such creation, alteration, combination or termination shall require a simple majority vote of approval of the three houses of the World Parliament in joint session.

7.2.12 The World Parliament by absolute majority vote of the three houses in joint session may specify the creation of new departments or agencies of ministerial status in the World Administration, or may direct the World Executive to alter, combine, or terminate existing departments or agencies of ministerial status.

7.2.13 The Presidium and the World Executive may not create, establish or maintain any administrative or executive department or agency for the purpose of circumventing control by the World Parliament.

Section 7.3   Departments of the World Administration

7.3.1 Disarmament & War Prevention.

7.3.2 Population.

7.3.3 Food and Agriculture.

7.3.4 Water Supplies and Waterways.

7.3.5 Health and Nutrition.

7.3.6 Education.

7.3.7 Cultural Diversity and the Arts.

7.3.8 Habitat and Settlements.

7.3.9 Environment and Ecology.

7.3.10 World Resources.

7.3.11 Oceans and Seabeds.

7.3.12 Atmosphere and Space.

7.3.13 Energy.

7.3.14 Science and Technology.

7.3.15 Genetic Research & Engineering.

7.3.16 Labor and Income.

7.3.17 Economic & Social Development.

7.3.18 Commerce & Industry

7.3.19 Transportation and Travel.

7.3.20 Multi-National Corporations.

7.3.21 Communications & Information.

7.3.22 Human Rights.

7.3.23 Distributive Justice.

7.3.24 World Service Corps.

7.3.25 World Territories, Capitals & Parks.

7.3.26 Exterior Relations.

7.3.27 Democratic Procedures.

7.3.28 Revenue.

Article 8

The Integrative Complex

Section 8.1   Definition

8.1.1 Certain administrative, research, planning and facilitative agencies of the World Government which are particularly essential for the satisfactory functioning of all or most aspects of the World Government, shall be designated as the Integrative Complex. The Integrative Complex shall include the agencies listed under this section, with the proviso that other such agencies may be added upon recommendation of the Presidium followed by decision of the World Parliament.

8.1.1.1 The World Civil Service Administration.

8.1.1.2 The World Boundaries and Elections Administration.

8.1.1.3 The Institute on Governmental Procedures and World Problems.

8.1.1.4 The Agency for Research and Planning.

8.1.1.5 The Agency for Technological and Environmental Assessment.

8.1.1.6 The World Financial Administration.

8.1.1.7 Commission for Legislative Review.

8.1.2 Each agency of the Integrative Complex shall be headed by a Cabinet Minister and a Senior Administrator, or by a Vice President and a Senior Administrator, together with a Commission as provided hereunder. The rules of procedure for each agency shall be decided by majority decision of the Commission members together with the Administrator and the Minister or Vice President.

8.1.3 The World Parliament may at any time define further the responsibilities, functioning and organization of the several agencies of the Integrative Complex, consistent with the provisions of Article 8 and other provisions of the World Constitution.

8.1.4 Each agency of the Integrative Complex shall make an annual report to the World Parliament and to the Presidium.

Section 8.2   The World Civil Service Administration

8.2.1 The functions of the World Civil Service Administration shall be the following, but not limited thereto:

8.2.1.1 To formulate and define standards, qualifications, tests, examinations and salary scales for the personnel of all organs, departments, bureaus, offices, commissions and agencies of the World Government, in conformity with the provisions of this World Constitution and requiring approval by the Presidium and Executive Cabinet, subject to review and approval by the World Parliament.

8.2.1.2 To establish rosters or lists of competent personnel for all categories of personnel to be appointed or employed in the service of the World Government.

8.2.1.3 To select and employ upon request by any government organ, department, bureau, office, institute, commission, agency or authorized official, such competent personnel as may be needed and authorized, except for those positions which are made elective or appointive under provisions of the World Constitution or by specific legislation of the World Parliament.

8.2.2 The World Civil Service Administration shall be headed by a ten member commission in addition to the Cabinet Minister or Vice President and Senior Administrator. The Commission shall be composed of one commissioner from each of ten World Electoral and Administrative Magna-Regions. The persons to serve as Commissioners shall be nominated by the House of Counsellors and then appointed by the Presidium for five year terms. Commissioners may serve consecutive terms.

Section 8.3   The World Boundaries and Elections Administration

8.3.1 The functions of the World Boundaries and Elections Administration shall include the following, but not limited thereto:

8.3.1.1 To define the boundaries for the basic World Electoral and Administrative Districts, the World Electoral and Administrative Regions and Magna-Regions, and the Continental Divisions, for submission to the World Parliament for approval by legislative action.

8.3.1.2 To make periodic adjustments every ten or five years, as needed, of the boundaries for the World Electoral and Administrative Districts, the World Electoral and Administrative Regions and Magna-Regions, and of the Continental Divisions, subject to approval by the World Parliament.

8.3.1.3 To define the detailed procedures for the nomination and election of Members of the World Parliament to the House of Peoples and to the House of Counsellors, subject to approval by the World Parliament.

8.3.1.4 To conduct the elections for Members of the World Parliament to the House of Peoples and to the House of Counsellors.

8.3.1.5 Before each World Parliamentary Election, to prepare Voters' Information Booklets which shall summarize major current public issues, and shall list each candidate for elective office together with standard information about each candidate, and give space for each candidate to state his or her views on the defined major issues as well as on any other major issue of choice; to include information on any initiatives or referendums which are to be voted upon; to distribute the Voters' Information Booklets for each World Electoral District, or suitable group of Districts; and to obtain the advice of the Institute on Governmental Procedures and World Problems, the Agency for Research and Planning, and the Agency for Technological and Environmental Assessment in preparing the booklets.

8.3.1.6 To define the rules for world political parties, subject to approval by the World Parliament, and subject to review and recommendations of the World Ombudsmus.

8.3.1.7 To define the detailed procedures for legislative initiative and referendum by the Citizens of Earth, and to conduct voting on supra- national or global initiatives and referendums in conjuction with world parliamentary elections.

8.3.1.8 To conduct plebiscites when requested by other Organs of the World Government, and to make recommendations for the settlement of boundary disputes.

8.3.1.9 To conduct a global census every five years, and to prepare and maintain complete demographic analyses for Earth.

8.3.2 The World Boundaries and Elections Administration shall be headed by a ten member commission in addition to the Senior Administrator and the Cabinet Minister or Vice President. The commission shall be composed of one commissioner each from ten World Electoral and Administrative Magna-Regions. The persons to serve as commissioners shall be nominated by the House of Counsellors and then appointed by the World Presidium for five year terms. Commissioners may serve consecutive terms.

Section 8.4   Institute on Governmental Procedures and World Problems

8.4.1 The functions of the Institute on Governmental Procedures and World Problems shall include the following, but not limited thereto:

8.4.1.1 To prepare and conduct courses of information, education and training for all personnel in the service of the World Government, including Members of the World Parliament and of all other elective, appointive and civil service personnel, so that every person in the service of the World Government may have a better understanding of the functions, structure, procedures and inter-relationships of the various organs, departments, bureaus, offices, institutes, commissions, agencies and other parts of the World Government.

8.4.1.2 To prepare and conduct courses and seminars for information, education, discussion, updating and new ideas in all areas of world problems, particularly for Members of the World Parliament and of the World Executive, and for the chief personnel of all organs, departments and agencies of the World Government, but open to all in the service of the World Government.

8.4.1.3 To bring in qualified persons from private and public universities, colleges and research and action organizations of many countries, as well as other qualified persons, to lecture and to be resource persons for the courses and seminars organized by the Institute on Governmental Procedures and World Problems.

8.4.1.4 To contract with private or public universities and colleges or other agencies to conduct courses and seminars for the Institute.

8.4.2 The Institute on Governmental Procedures and World Problems shall be supervised by a ten member commission in addition to the Senior Administrator and Cabinet Minister or Vice President. The commission shall be composed of one commissioner each to be named by the House of Peoples, the House of Nations, the House of Counsellors, the Presidium, the Collegium of World Judges, The World

Ombudsmus, The World Attorneys General Office, the Agency for Research and Planning, the Agency for Technological and Environmental Assessment, and the World Financial Administration. Commissioners shall serve five year terms, and may serve consecutive terms.

Section 8.5   The Agency for Research and Planning

8.5.1 The functions of the Agency for Research and Planning shall be as follows, but not limited thereto:

8.5.1.1 To serve the World Parliament, the World Executive, the World Administration, and other organs, departments and agencies of the World Government in any matter requiring research and planning within the competence of the agency.

8.5.1.2 To prepare and maintain a comprehensive inventory of world resources.

8.5.1.3 To prepare comprehensive long-range plans for the development, conservation, recycling and equitable sharing of the resources of Earth for the benefit of all people on

Earth, subject to legislative action by the World Parliament.

8.5.1.4 To prepare and maintain a comprehensive list and description of all world problems, including their inter-relationships, impact time projections and proposed solutions, together with bibliographies.

8.5.1.5 To do research and help prepare legislative measures at the request of any Member of the World Parliament or of any committee of any House of the World Parliament.

8.5.1.6 To do research and help prepare proposed legislation or proposed legislative programs and schedules at the request of the Presidium or Executive Cabinet or of any Cabinet Minister.

8.5.1.7 To do research and prepare reports at the request of any other organ, department or agency of the World Government.

8.5.1.8 To enlist the help of public and private universities, colleges, research agencies, and other associations and organizations for various research and planning projects.

8.5.1.9 To contract with public and private universities, colleges, research agencies and other organizations for the preparation of specific reports, studies and proposals.

8.5.1.10 To maintain a comprehensive World Library for the use of all Members of the World Parliament, and for the use of all other officials and persons in the service of the World Government, as well as for public information.

8.5.2 The Agency for Research and Planning shall be supervised by a ten member commission in addition to the Senior Administrator and Cabinet Minister or Vice President. The commission shall be composed of one commissioner each to be named by the House of Peoples, the House of Nations, the House of Counsellors, the Presidium, the Collegium of World Judges, the Office of World Attorneys General, World Ombudsmus, the Agency for Technological and Environmental Assessment, the Institute on Governmental Procedures and World Problems, and the World Financial Administration. Commissioners shall serve five year terms, and may serve consecutive terms.

Section 8.6   The Agency for Technological and Environmental Assessment

8.6.1 The functions of the agency for Technological and Environmental Assessment shall include the following, but not limited thereto:

   8.6.1.1 To establish and maintain a registration and description of all significant technological innovations, together with impact projections.

   8.6.1.2 To examine, analyze and assess the impacts and consequences of technological innovations which may have either significant beneficial or significant harmful or dangerous consequences for human life or for the ecology of life on Earth, or which may require particular regulations or prohibitions to prevent or eliminate dangers or to assure benefits.

   8.6.1.3 To examine, analyze and assess environmental and ecological problems, in particular the environmental and ecological problems which may result from any intrusions or changes of the environment or ecological relationships which may be caused by technological innovations, processes of resource development, patterns of human settlements, the production of energy, patterns of economic and industrial development, or other man-made intrusions and changes of the environment, or which may result from natural causes.

8.6.1.4 To maintain a global monitoring network to measure possible harmful effects of technological innovations and environmental disturbances so that corrective measures can be designed.

8.6.1.5 To prepare recommendations based on technological and environmental analyses and assessments, which can serve as guides to the World Parliament, the World Executive, the World Administration, the Agency for Research and Planning, and to the other organs, departments and agencies of the World Government, as well as to individuals in the service of the World Government and to national and local governments and legislative bodies.

8.6.1.6 To enlist the voluntary or contractual aid and participation of private

and public universities, colleges, research institutions and other associations and organizations in the work
of technological and environmental
assessment.

8.6.1.7 To enlist the voluntary or contractual aid and participation of private and public universities and colleges, research institutions and other
organizations in devising and developing alternatives to harmful or
dangerous technologies and environmentally disruptive activities, and
in devising controls to assure beneficial results from technological innovations or to prevent harmful results from either technological innovations or environmental changes,
all subject to legislation for implementation by the World Parliament.

8.6.2 The Agency for Technological and Environmental Assessment shall be supervised by a ten member commission
in addition to the Senior Administrator and Cabinet Minister or Vice President.   The commission shall be composed of one commissioner from each of
ten World Electoral and Administrative
Magna-Regions.   The persons to serve
as commissioners shall be nominated by

the House of Counsellors, and then appointed by the World Presidium for five year terms. Commissioners may serve consecutive terms.

Section 8.7   The World Financial Administration

8.7.1 The functions of the World Financial Administration shall include the following, but not limited thereto:

8.7.1.1 To establish and operate the procedures for the collection of revenues for the World Government, pursuant to legislation by the World Parliament, inclusive of taxes, globally accounted social and public costs, licenses, fees, revenue sharing arrangements, income derived from supra-national public enterprises or projects or resource developments, and all other sources.

8.7.1.2 To operate a Planetary Accounting Office, and thereunder to make cost/benefit studies and reports of the functioning and activities of the World Government and of its several organs, departments, branches, bureaus, offices, commissions, institutes, agencies and other parts or projects. In making such studies and reports, account shall be taken not only of direct financial costs and benefits, but also of human, social, environmental, indirect, long-term and other costs and benefits, and of actual or possible hazards and damages. Such studies and reports shall also be designed to uncover any wastes, inefficiencies, misapplications, corruptions, diversions, unnecessary costs, and other possible irregularities.

8.7.1.3 To make cost/benefit studies and reports at the request of any House or committee of the World Parliament, and of the Presidium, the Executive Cabinet, the World Ombudsmus, the Office of World Attorneys General, the World Supreme Court, or of any administrative department or any agency of the Integrative Complex, as well as upon its own initiative.

8.7.1.4 To operate a Planetary Comptrollers Office and thereunder to supervise the disbursement of the funds of the World Government for all purposes, projects and activities duly authorized by this World Constitution, the

World Parliament, the World Executive, and other organs, departments and agencies of the World Government.

8.7.1.5 To establish and operate a Planetary Banking System, making the transition to a common global currency, under the terms of specific legislation passed by the World Parliament.

8.7.1.6 Pursuant to specific legislation enacted by the World Parliament, and in conjunction with the Planetary Banking System, to establish and implement the procedures of a Planetary Monetary and Credit System based upon useful productive capacity and performance, both in goods and services. Such a monetary and credit system shall be designed for use within the Planetary Banking System for the financing of the activities and projects of the World Government, and for all other financial purposes approved by the World Parliament, without requiring the payment of interest on bonds, investments or other claims of financial ownership or debt.

8.7.1.7 To establish criteria for the extension of financial credit based upon such considerations as people available to work, usefulness, cost/benefit accounting, human and social values, environmental health and esthetics, minimizing disparities, integrity, competent management, appropriate technology, potential production and performance.

8.7.1.8 To establish and operate a Planetary Insurance System in areas of world need which transcend national boundaries and in accordance with legislation passed by the World Parliament.

8.7.1.9 To assist the Presidium as may be requested in the technical preparation of budgets for the operation of the World Government.

8.7.2 The World Financial Administration shall be supervised by a commission of ten members, together with a Senior Administrator and a Cabinet Minister or Vice President. The commission shall be composed of one commissioner each to be named by the House of Peoples, the House of Nations, the House of Counsellors, the Presidium, the Collegium of World Judges, the Office of Attorneys General, the World Ombudsmus, the Agency for Research and Planning, the Agency for Technological and Environmental Assessment, and the Institute on Governmental Procedures and World Problems.   Commissioners shall serve terms of five years, and may serve consecutive terms.

Section 8.8   Commission for Legistlative Review

8.8.1 The functions of the Commission for Legislative Review shall be to examine World Legislation and World Laws which the World Parliament enacts or adopts from the previous Body of International Law for the purpose of analyzing whether any particular legislation or law has become obsolete or obstructive or defective in serving the purposes intended; and to make recommendations to the World Parliament accordingly for repeal or amendment or replacement.

8.8.2 The Commission for Legislative Review shall be composed of twelve members, including two each to be elected by the House of Peoples, the House of Nations, the House of Counsellors, the Collegium of World Judges, the World Ombudsmus and the Presidium. Members of the Commission shall serve terms of ten years, and may be re-elected to serve consecutive terms. One half of the Commission members after the Commission is first formed shall be elected every five years, with the first terms for one half of the members to be only five years.

Article 9

The World Judiciary

Section 9.1 Jurisdiction of the World Supreme Court

9.1.1 A World Supreme Court shall be established, together with such regional and district World Courts as may subsequently be found necessary. The World Supreme Court shall comprise a number of benches.

9.1.2 The World Supreme Court, together with such regional and district World Courts as may be established, shall have mandatory jurisdiction in all cases, actions, disputes, conflicts, violations of law, civil suits, guarantees of civil and human rights, con-

stitutional interpretations, and other litigations arising under the provisions of
this World Constitution, world legislation,
and the body of world law approved by
the World Parliament.

9.1.3 Decisions of the World Supreme Court
shall be binding on all parties involved in
all cases, actions and litigations brought
before any bench of the World Supreme
Court for settlement. Each bench of the
World Supreme Court shall constitute a
court of highest appeal, except when matters of extra-ordinary public importance
are assigned or transferred to the Superior
Tribunal of the World Supreme Court, as
provided in Section 5 of Article 9.

Section 9.2   Benches of the World
Supreme Court

The benches of the World Supreme Court and
their respective jurisdictions shall be as follows:

9.2.1 Bench for Human Rights: To deal with
issues of human rights arising under the
guarantee of civil and human rights provided by Article 12 of this World Constitution, and arising in pursuance of the provisions of Article 13 of this World Constitution, and arising otherwise under world

legislation and the body of world law approved by the World Parliament.

9.2.2 Bench for Criminal Cases: To deal with issues arising from the violation of world laws and world legislation by individuals, corporations, groups and associations, but not issues primarily concerned with human rights.

9.2.3 Bench for Civil Cases: To deal with issues involving civil law suits and disputes between individuals, corporations, groups and associations arising under world legislation and world law and the administration thereof.

9.2.4 Bench for Constitutional Cases: To deal with the interpretation of the World Constitution and with issues and actions arising in connection with the interpretation of the World Constitution.

9.2.5 Bench for International Conflicts: To deal with disputes, conflicts and legal contest arising between or among the nations which have joined in the Federation of Earth.

9.2.6 Bench for Public Cases: To deal with issues not under the jurisdiction of another bench arising from conflicts, disputes, civil suits or other legal contests between the World Government and corporations, groups or individuals, or between national governments and corporations, groups or individuals in cases involving world legislation and world law.

9.2.7 Appellate Bench: To deal with issues involving world legislation and world law which may be appealed from national courts; and to decide which bench to assign a case or action or litigation when a question or disagreement arises over the proper jurisdiction.

9.2.8 Advisory Bench: To give opinions upon request on any legal question arising under world law or world legislation, exclusive of contests or actions involving interpretation of the World Constitution. Advisory opinions may be requested by any House or committee of the World Parliament, by the Presidium, any Administrative Department, the Office of World Attorneys General, the World Ombudsmus, or by any agency of the Integrative Complex.

9.2.9 Other benches may be established, combined or terminated upon recommendation of the Collegium of World Judges with approval by the World Parliament; but benches number one through eight may not be combined nor terminated except by amendment of this World Constitution.

Section 9.3   Seats of the World Supreme Court

9.3.1 The primary seat of the World Supreme Court and all benches shall be the same as for the location of the Primary World Capital and for the location of the World Parliament and the World Executive.

9.3.2 Continental seats of the World Supreme Court shall be established in the four secondary capitals of the World Government located in four different Continental Divisions of Earth, as provided in Article 15.

9.3.3 The following permanent benches of the World Supreme Court shall be established both at the primary seat and at each of the continental seats: Human Rights, Criminal Cases, Civil Cases, and Public Cases.

9.3.4 The following permanent benches of the World Supreme Court shall be located only at the primary seat of the World Supreme Court: Constitutional Cases, International Conflicts, Appellate Bench, and Advisory Bench.

9.3.5 Benches which are located permanently only at the primary seat of the World Supreme Court may hold special sessions at the other continental seats of the World Supreme Court when necessary, or may establish continental circuits if needed.

9.3.6 Benches of the World Supreme Court which have permanent continental locations may hold special sessions at other locations when needed, or may establish regional circuits if needed.

Section 9.4   The Collegium of World Judges

9.4.1 A Collegium of World Judges shall be established by the World Parliament. The Collegium shall consist of a minimum of twenty member judges, and may be expanded as needed but not to exceed sixty members.

9.4.2 The World Judges to compose the Collegium of World Judges shall be nominated by the House of Counsellors and shall be elected by plurality vote of the three Houses of the World Parliament in joint session. The House of Counsellors shall nominate between two and three times the number of world judges to be elected at any one time. An equal number of World Judges shall be elected from each of ten World Electoral and Administrative Magna-Regions, if not immediately then by rotation.

9.4.3 The term of office for a World Judge shall be ten years. Successive terms may be served without limit.

9.4.4 The Collegium of World Judges shall elect a Presiding Council of World Judges, consisting of a Chief Justice and four Associate Chief Justices. One member of the Presiding Council of World Judges shall be elected from each of five Continental Divisions of Earth. Members of the Presiding Council of World Judges shall serve five year terms on the Presiding Council, and may serve two successive terms, but not two successive terms as Chief Justice.

9.4.5 The Presiding Council of World Judges shall assign all World Judges, including themselves, to the several benches of the World Supreme Court. Each bench for a sitting at each location shall have a minimum of three World Judges, except that the number of World Judges for benches on Continental Cases and International Conflicts, and the Appellate Bench, shall be no less than five.

9.4.6 The member judges of each bench at each location shall choose annually a Presiding Judge, who may serve two successive terms.

9.4.7 The members of the several benches may be reconstituted from time to time as may seem desirable or necessary upon the decision of the Presiding Council of World Judges. Any decision to re-constitute a bench shall be referred to a vote of the entire Collegium of World Judges by request of any World Judge.

9.4.8 Any World Judge may be removed from office for cause by an absolute two thirds majority vote of the three Houses of the World Parliament in joint session.

9.4.9 Qualifications for Judges of the World Supreme Court shall be at least ten years of legal or juristic experience, minimum age of thirty years, and evident competence in world law and the humanities.

9.4.10 The salaries, expenses, remunerations and prerogatives of the World Judges shall be determined by the World Parliament, and shall be reviewed every five years, but shall not be changed to the disadvantage of any World Judge during a term of office. All members of the Collegium of World

Judges shall receive the same salaries, except that additional compensation may be given to the Presiding Council of World Judges.

9.4.11 Upon recommendation by the Collegium of World Judges, the World Parliament shall have the authority to establish regional and district world courts below the World Supreme Court, and to establish the jurisdictions thereof, and the procedures for appeal to the World Supreme Court or to the several benches thereof.

9.4.12 The detailed rules of procedure for the functioning of the World Supreme Court, the Collegium of World Judges, and for each bench of the World Supreme Court, shall be decided and amended by absolute majority vote of the Collegium of World Judges.

Section 9.5   The Superior Tribunal of World Supreme Court

9.5.1 A Superior Tribunal of the World Supreme Court shall be established to take cases which are considered to be of extraordinary public importance. The Superior Tribunal for any calendar year shall consist of the Presiding Council of World

Judges together with one World Judge named by the Presiding Judge of each bench of the World Court sitting at the primary seat of the World Supreme Court. The composition of the Superior Tribunal may be continued unchanged for a second year by decision of the Presiding Council of World Judges.

9.5.2 Any party to any dispute, issue, case or litigation coming under the jurisdiction of the World Supreme Court, may apply to any particular bench of the World Supreme Court or to the Presiding Council of World Judges for the assignment or transfer of the case to the Superior Tribunal on the grounds of extra-ordinary public importance. If the application is granted, the case shall be heard and disposed of by the Superior Tribunal. Also, any bench taking any particular case, if satisfied that the case is of extra-ordinary public importance, may of its own discretion transfer the case to the Superior Tribunal.

Article 10

The Enforcement System

Section 10.1　Basic Principles

10.1.1 The enforcement of world law and world legislation shall apply directly to individual, and individuals shall be held responsible for compliance with world law and world legislation regardless of whether the individuals are acting in their own capacity or as agents or officials of governments at any level or of the institutions of governments, or as agents or officials of corporations, organizations, associations or groups of any kind.

10.1.2 When world law or world legislation or decisions of the world courts are violated, the Enforcement System shall operate to identify and apprehend the individuals responsible for violations.

10.1.3 Any enforcement action shall not violate the civil and human rights guaranteed under this World Constitution.

10.1.4 The enforcement of world law and world legislation shall be carried out in the context of a non-military world federation wherein all member nations shall disarm as a condition for joining and benefiting from the world federation, subject to Article 17, Sec. 3.8 and 4.6 The Federation of Earth and World Government under this World Constitution shall neither keep nor use weapons of mass destruction.

10.1.5 Those agents of the enforcement system whose function shall be to apprehend and bring to court violators of world law and world legislation shall be equipped only with such weapons as are appropriate for the apprehension of the individuals responsible for violations.

10.1.6 The enforcement of world law and world legislation under this World Constitution shall be conceived and developed primarily as the processes of effective design and administration of world law and world legislation to serve the welfare of all people on Earth, with equity and justice for all, in which the resources of Earth and the funds and the credits of the World Government are used only to serve peaceful human needs, and none used for weapons of mass destruction or for war making capabilities.

Section 10.2   The Structure for Enforcement: World Attorneys General

10.2.1 The Enforcement System shall be headed by an Office of World Attorneys General and a Commission of Regional World Attorneys.

10.2.2 The Office of World Attorneys General shall be comprised of five members, one of whom shall be designated as the World Attorney General and the other four shall each be designated an Associate World Attorney General.

10.2.3 The Commission of Regional World Attorneys shall consist of twenty Regional

World Attorneys.

10.2.4 The members to compse the Office of World Attorneys General shall be nominated by the House of Counsellors, with three nominees from each Continental Division of Earth. One member of the Office shall be elected from each of five Continental Divisions by plurality vote of the three houses of the World Parliament in joint session.

10.2.5 The term of office for a member of the Office of World Attorneys General shall be ten years. A member may serve two consecutive terms. The position of World Attorney General shall rotate every two years among the five members of the Office. The order of rotation shall be decided among the five members of the Office.

10.2.6 The Office of World Attorneys General shall nominate members for the Commission of twenty Regional World Attorneys from the twenty World Electoral and Administrative Regions, with between two and three nominees submitted for each Region. From these nominations, the three Houses of the World Parliament in joint session shall elect one Regional World Attorney from each of the twenty Regions. Regional World Attorneys shall serve terms of five years, and may serve three consecutive terms.

10.2.7 Each Regional World Attorney shall organize and be in charge of an Office of Regional World Attorney. Each Associate World Attorney General shall supervise five Offices of Regional World Attorneys.

10.2.8 The staff to carry out the work of enforcement, in addition to the five members of the Office of World Attorneys General and the twenty Regional World Attorneys, shall be selected from civil service lists, and shall be organized for the following functions:

10.2.8.1 Investigation.

10.2.8.2 Apprehension and arrest.

10.2.8.3 Prosecution.

10.2.8.4 Remedies and correction.

10.2.8.5 Conflict resolution.

10.2.9 Qualifications for a member of the Office of World Attorneys General and for the Regional World Attorneys shall be at least thirty years of age, at least seven years legal experience, and education in law and the humanities.

10.2.10 The World Attorney General, the Associate World Attorneys General, and the

Regional World Attorneys shall at all times be responsible to the World Parliament. Any member of the Office of World Attorneys General and any Regional World Attorney can be removed from office for cause by a simple majority vote of the three Houses of the World Parliament in joint session.

Section 10.3   The World Police

10.3.1 That section of the staff of the Office of World Attorneys General and of the Offices of Regional World Attorneys responsible for the apprehension and arrest of violators of world law and world legislation, shall be designated as World Police.

10.3.2 Each regional staff of the World Police shall be headed by a Regional World Police Captain, who shall be appointed by the Regional World Attorney.

10.3.3 The Office of World Attorneys General shall appoint a World Police Supervisor, to be in charge of those activities which transcend regional boundaries. The World Police Supervisor shall direct the Regional World Police Captains in any actions which require coordinated or joint action transcending regional boundaries, and shall direct any action which requires initiation or direction from the Office of World Attorneys General.

10.3.4 Searches and arrests to be made by World Police shall be made only upon warrants issued by the Office of World Attorneys General or by a Regional World Attorney.

10.3.5 World Police shall be armed only with weapons appropriate for the apprehension of the individuals responsible for violation of world law.

10.3.6 Employment in the capacity of World Police Captain and World Police Supervisor shall be limited to ten years.

10.3.7 The World Police Supervisor and any Regional World Police Captain may be removed from office for cause by decision of the Office of World Attorneys General or by absolute majority vote of the three Houses of the World Parliament in joint session.

Section 10.4   The Means of Enforcement

10.4.1 Non-military means of enforcement of world law and world legislation shall be developed by the World Parliament and by the Office of World Attorneys General in consultation with the Commission of Regional World Attorneys, the Collegium of World Judges, the World Presidium, and the World Ombudsmus. The actual means of enforcement shall require legislation by the World Parliament.

10.4.2 Non-military means of enforcement which can be developed may include: Denial of financial credit; denial of material resources and personnel; revocation of licenses, charters, or corporate rights; impounding of equipment; fines and damage payments; performance of work to rectify damages; imprisonment or isolation; and other means appropriate to the specific situations.

10.4.3 To cope with situations of potential or actual riots, insurrection and resort to armed violence, particular strategies and methods shall be developed by the World Parliament and by the Office of World Attorneys General in consultation with the Commission of Regional World Attorneys, the collegium of World Judges, the Presidium and the World Ombudsmus. Such strategies and methods shall require enabling legislation by the World Parliament where required in addition to the specific provisions of this World Constitution.

10.4.4 A basic condition for preventing outbreaks of violence which the Enforcement System shall facilitate in every way possible, shall be to assure a fair hearing under non-violent circumstances for any person or group having a grievance, and likewise to assure a fair opportunity for a just settlement of any grievance with due regard for the rights and welfare of all concerned.

Article 11

The World Ombudsmus

Section 11.1   Functions and Powers of the World Ombudsmus

The functions and powers of the World Ombudsmus, as public defender, shall include the following:

11.1.1 To protect the People of Earth and all individuals against violations or neglect of universal human and civil rights which are stipulated in Article 12 and other sections of this World Constitution.

11.1.2 To protect the People of Earth against violations of this World Constitution by any official or agency of the World Government, including both elected and appointed officials or public employees regardless of organ, department, office, agency or rank.

11.1.3 To press for the implementation of the Directive Principles for the World Government as defined in Article 13 of this World Constitution.

11.1.4 To promote the welfare of the people of Earth by seeking to assure that conditions of social justice and of minimizing disparities are achieved in the implementation and administration of world legislation and world law.

11.1.5 To keep on the alert for perils to humanity arising from technological innovations, environmental disruptions and other diverse sources, and to launch initiatives for correction or prevention of such perils.

11.1.6 To ascertain that the administration of otherwise proper laws, ordinances and procedures of the World Government do not result in unforseen injustices or inequities, or become stultified in bureaucracy or the details of administration.

11.1.7 To receive and hear complaints, grievances or requests for aid from any person, group, organization, association, body politic or agency concerning any matter which comes within the purview of the World Ombudsmus.

11.1.8 To request the Office of World Attorneys General or any Regional World Attorney to initiate legal actions or court proceedings whenever and wherever considered necessary or desirable in the view of the World Ombudsmus.

11.1.9 To directly initiate legal actions and court proceedings whenever the World Ombudsmus deems necessary.

11.1.10 To review the functioning of the departments, bureaus, offices, commissions, institutes, organs and agencies of the World Government to ascertain whether the procedures of the World government are adequately fulfilling their purposes and serving the welfare of humanity in optimum fashion, and to make recommendations for improvements.

11.1.11 To present an annual report to the World Parliament and to the Presidium on the activities of the World Ombudsmus, together with any recommendations for legislative measures to improve the functioning of the World Government for the purpose of better serving the welfare of the People of Earth.

Section 11.2   Composition of the World Ombudsmus

11.2.1 The World Ombudsmus shall be headed by a Council of World Ombudsen of five members, one of whom shall be designated as Principal World Ombudsan, while the other four shall each be designated as an Associate World Ombudsan.

11.2.2 Members to compose the Council of World Ombudsen shall be nominated by the House of Counsellors, with three nominees from each Continental Division of Earth. One member of the Council shall be elected from each of five Continental Divisions by plurality vote of the three Houses of the World Parliament in joint session.

11.2.3 The term of office for a World Ombudsan shall be ten years. A World Ombudsan may serve two successive terms. The position of Principal World Ombudsan shall be rotated every two years. The order of rotation shall be determined by the Council of World Ombudsen.

11.2.4 The Council of World Ombudsen shall be assisted by a Commission of World Advocates of twenty members. Members for the Commission of World Advocates shall be nominated by the Council of World Ombudsen from twenty World Electoral and Administrative Regions, with between two and three nominees submitted for each Region. One World Advocate shall be elected from each of the twenty World Electoral and Administrative Regions by the three Houses of the World Parliament in joint session. World Advocates shall serve terms of five years, and may serve a maximum of four successive terms.

11.2.5 The Council of World Ombudsen shall establish twenty regional offices, in addition to the principal world office at the primary seat of the World Government. The twenty regional offices of the World Ombudsmus shall parallel the organization of the twenty Offices of Regional World Attorney.

11.2.6 Each regional office of the World Ombudsmus shall be headed by a World Advocate. Each five regional offices of the

World Ombudmus shall be supervised by
an Associate World Ombudsan.

11.2.7 Any World Ombudsan and any World
Advocate may be removed from office for
cause by an absolute majority vote of the
three Houses of the World Parliament in
joint session.

11.2.8 Staff members for the World Ombudsmus and for each regional office of
the World Ombudsmus shall be selected
and employed from civil service lists.

11.2.9 Qualifications for World Ombudsan
and for World Advocate shall be at least
thirty years of age, at least five years legal experience, and education in law and
other relevant education.

Article 12

Bill of Rights for the Citizens of Earth

12.1 Equal rights for all citizens of the Federation of Earth, with no discrimination on grounds of race, color, caste, nationality, sex, religion, political affiliation, property, or social status.

12.2 Equal protection and application of world legislation and world laws for all citizens of the Federation of Earth.

12.3 Freedom of thought and conscience, speech, press, writing, communication, expression, publication, broadcasting, telecasting, and cinema, except as an overt part of or incitement to violence, armed riot or insurrection.

12.4 Freedom of assembly, association, organization, petition and peaceful demonstration.

12.5 Freedom to vote without duress, and freedom for political organization and campaigning without censorship or recrimination.

12.6 Freedom to profess, practice and promote religion or religious beliefs or no religion or religious belief.

12.7 Freedom to profess and promote political beliefs or no political beliefs.

12.8 Freedom for investigation, research and reporting.

12.9 Freedom to travel without passport or visas or other forms of registration used to limit travel between, among or within nations.

12.10 Prohibition against slavery, peonage, involuntary servitude, and conscription of labor.

12.11 Prohibition against military conscription.

12.12 Safety of person from arbitrary or un-
reasonable arrest, detention, exile, search
or seizure; requirement of warrants for
searches and arrests.

12.13 Prohibition against physical or psycho-
logical duress or torture during any period of investigation, arrest, detention or
imprisonment, and against cruel or un-
usual punishment.

12.14 Right of habeous corpus; no ex-post-
facto laws; no double jeopardy; right to
refuse self-incrimination or the incrimina-
tion of another.

12.15 Prohibition against private armies
and paramilitary organizations as being
threats to the common peace and safety.

12.16 Safety of property from arbitrary
seizure; protection against exercise of
the power of eminent domain without
reasonable compensation.

12.17 Right to family planning and free public
assistance to achieve family planning ob-
jectives.

12.18 Right of privacy of person, family and
association; prohibition against surveil-
lance as a means of political control.

Article 13

Directive Principles for the Earth Federation

It shall be the aim of the World Government to secure certain other rights for all inhabitants within the Federation of Earth, but without immediate guarantee of universal achievement and enforcement. These rights are defined as Directive Principles, obligating the World Government to pursue every reasonable means for universal realization and implementation, and shall include the following:

13.1 Equal opportunity for useful employment for everyone, with wages or remuneration sufficient to assure human dignity.

13.2 Freedom of choice in work, occupation, employment or profession.

13.3 Full access to information and to the accumulated knowledge of the human race.

13.4 Free and adequate public education available to everyone, extending to the pre-university level; Equal opportunities for elementary and higher education for all persons; equal opportunity for continued education for all persons throughout life; the right of any person or parent to choose a private educational institution at any time.

13.5 Free and adequate public health services and medical care available to everyone throughout life under conditions of free choice.

13.6 Equal opportunity for leisure time for everyone; better distribution of the work load of society so that every person may have equitable leisure time opportunities.

13.7 Equal opportunity for everyone to enjoy the benefits of scientific and technological discoveries and developments.

13.8 Protection for everyone against the hazards and perils of technological innovations and developments.

13.9 Protection of the natural environment which is the common heritage of humanity against pollution, ecological disruption or damage which could imperil life or lower the quality of life.

13.10 Conservation of those natural resources of Earth which are limited so that present and future generations may continue to enjoy life on the planet Earth.

13.11 Assurance for everyone of adequate housing, of adequate and nutritious food supplies, of safe and adequate water supplies, of pure air with protection of oxygen supplies and the ozone layer, and in general for the continuance of an environment which can sustain healthy living for all.

13.12 Assure to each child the right to the full realization of his or her potential.

13.13 Social Security for everyone to relieve the hazards of unemployment, sickness, old age, family circumstances, disability, catastrophies of nature, and technological change, and to allow retirement with sufficient lifetime income for living under conditions of human dignity during older age.

13.14 Rapid elimination of and prohibitions against technological hazards and man-made environmental disturbances which are found to create dangers to life on Earth.

13.15 Implementation of intensive programs to discover, develop and institute safe alternatives and practical substitutions for technologies which must be eliminated and prohibited because of hazards and dangers to life.

13.16 Encouragement for cultural diversity; encouragement for decentralized administration.

13.17 Freedom for peaceful self-determination for minorities, refugees and dissenters.

13.18 Freedom for change of residence to anywhere on Earth conditioned by provisions for temporary sanctuaries in events of large numbers of refugees, stateless persons, or mass migrations.

13.19 Prohibition against the death penalty.

Article 14

Safeguards and Reservations

Section 14.1 Certain Safeguards

The World Government shall operate to secure for all nations and peoples within the Federation of Earth the safeguards which are defined hereunder:

14.1.1 Guarantee that full faith and credit shall be given to the public acts, records, legislation and judicial proceedings of the member nations within the Federation of Earth, consistent with the several provisions of this World Constitution.

14.1.2 Assure freedom of choice within the

member nations and countries of the Federation of Earth to determine their internal political, economic and social systems consistent with the guarantees and protections given under this World Constitution to assure civil liberties and human rights and a safe environment for life, and otherwise consistent with the several provisions of this World Constitution.

14.1.3 Grant the right of asylum within the Federation of Earth for persons who may seek refuge from countries or nations which are not yet included within the Federation of Earth.

14.1.4 Grant the right of individuals and groups, after the Federation of Earth includes 90 percent of the territory of Earth, to peacefully leave the hegemony of the Federation of Earth and to live in suitable territory set aside by the Federation neither restricted nor protected by the World Government, provided that such territory does not extend beyond five percent of Earth's habitable territory, is kept completely disarmed and not used as a base for inciting violence or insurrection within or against the Federation of Earth or any member nation, and is kept free of acts of environmental or technological damage which seriously affect Earth outside such territory.

Section 14.2   Reservation of Powers

The powers not delegated to the World Government by this World Constitution shall be reserved to the nations of the Federation of Earth and to the people of Earth.

Article 15

World Federal Zones and the World Capitals

Section 15.1   Word Federal Zones

15.1.1 Twenty World Federal Zones shall be established within the twenty World Electoral and Administrative Regions, for the purposes of the location of the several organs of the World Government and of the administrative departments, the world courts, the offices of the Regional World Attorneys, the offices of the World Advocates, and for the location of other branches, departments, institutes, offices, bureaus, commissions, agencies and parts of the World Government.

15.1.2 The World Federal Zones shall be established as the needs and resources of the World Government develop and expand. World Federal Zones shall be established first within each of five Continental Divisions.

15.1.3 The location and administration of the World Federal Zones, including the first five, shall be determined by the World Parliament.

Section 15.2   The World Capitals

15.2.1 Five World Capitals shall be established in each of five Continental Divisions of Earth, to be located in each of the five World Federal Zones which are established first as provided in Article 15 of this World Constitution.

15.2.2 One of the World Capitals shall be designated by the World Parliament as the Primary World Capital, and the other four shall be designated as Secondary World Capitals.

15.2.3 The primary seats of all organs of the World Government shall be located in the Primary World Capital, and other major seats of the several organs of the World

Government shall be located in the Secondary World Capitals.

Section 15.3 Locational Procedures

15.3.1 Choices for location of the twenty World Federal Zones and for the five World Capitals shall be proposed by the Presidium, and then shall be decided by a simple majority vote of the three Houses of the World Parliament in joint session. The Presidium shall offer choices of two or three locations in each of the twenty World Electoral and Administrative Regions to be World Federal Zones, and shall offer two alternative choices for each of the five World Capitals.

15.3.2 The Presidium in consultation with the Executive Cabinet shall then propose which of the five World Capitals shall be the Primary World Capital, to be decided by a simply majority vote of the three Houses of the World Parliament in joint session.

15.3.3 Each organ of the World Government shall decide how best to apportion and organize its functions and activities among the five World Capitals, and among the twenty World Federal Zones, subject to specific directions from the World Parliament.

15.3.4 The World Parliament may decide to rotate its sessions among the five World Capitals, and if so, to decide the procedure for rotation.

15.3.5 For the first two operative stages of World Government as defined in Article 17, and for the Provisional World Government as defined in Article 19, a provisional location may be selected for the Primary World Capital. The provisional location need not be continued as a permanent location.

15.3.6 Any World Capital or World Federal Zone may be relocated by an absolute two-thirds majority vote of the three Houses of the World Parliament in joint session.

15.3.7 Additional World Federal Zones may be designated if found necessary by proposal of the Presidium and approval by an absolute majority vote of the three Houses of the World Parliament in joint session.

Article 16

World Territories and Exterior Relations

Section 16.1   World Territory

16.1.1 Those areas of the Earth and Earth's moon which are not under the jurisdiction of existing nations at the time of forming the Federation of Earth, or which are not reasonably within the province of national ownership and administration, or which are declared to be World Territory subsequent to establishment of the Federation of Earth, shall be designated as World Territory and shall belong to all of the people of Earth.

16.1.2 The administration of World Territory shall be determined by the World Parliament and implemented by the World Executive, and shall apply to the following areas:

16.1.2.1 All oceans and seas having an international or supra-national character, together with the seabeds and resources thereof, beginning at a distance of twenty kilometers offshore, excluding inland seas of traditional national ownership.

16.1.2.2 Vital straits, channels, and canals.

16.1.2.3 The atmosphere enveloping Earth, beginning at an elevation of one kilometer above the general surface of the land, excluding the depressions in areas of much variation in elevation.

16.1.2.4 Man-made satellites and Earth's moon.

16.1.2.5 Colonies which may choose the status of World Territory; non-independent territories under the trust administration of nations or of the United Nations; any islands or atolls which are unclaimed by any nation; independent lands or countries which choose the status of

World Territory; and disputed lands which choose the status of World Territory.

16.1.3 The residents of any World Territory, except designated World Federal Zones, shall have the right within reason to decide by plebiscite to become a self-governing nation within the Federation of Earth, either singly or in combination with other World Territories, or to unite with an existing nation with the Federation of Earth.

Section 16.2   Exterior Relations

16.2.1 The World Government shall maintain exterior relations with those nations of Earth which have not joined the Federation of Earth. Exterior relations shall be under the administration of the Presidium, subject at all times to specific instructions and approval by the World Parliament.

16.2.2 All treaties and agreements with nations remaining outside the Federation of Earth shall be negotiated by the Presidium and must be ratified by a simple majority vote of the three Houses of the World Parliament.

16.2.3 The World Government for the Federation of Earth shall establish and maintain peaceful relations with other planets and celestial bodies where and when it may become possible to establish communications with the possible inhabitants thereof.

16.2.4 All explorations into outer space, both within and beyond the solar system in which Planet Earth is located, shall be under the exclusive direction and control of the World Government, and shall be conducted in such manner as shall be determined by the World Parliament.

Article 17

Ratification and Implementation

Section 17.1   Ratification of the World Constitution

17.1.1 The World Constitution shall be transmitted to the General Assembly of the United Nations Organization and to each national government on Earth, with the request that the World Constitution be submitted to the national legislature of each nation for preliminary ratification and to the people of each nation for final ratification by popular referendum.

17.1.2 Preliminary ratification by a national

legislature shall be accomplished by simple majority vote of the national legislature.

17.1.3 Final ratification by the people shall be accomplished by a simple majority of votes cast in a popular referendum, provided that a minimum of twenty-five percent of eligible voters of age eighteen years and over have cast ballots within the nation or country or within World Electoral and Administrative Districts.

17.1.4 In the case of a nation without a national legislature, the head of the national government shall be requested to give preliminary ratification and to submit the World Constitution for final ratification by popular referendum.

17.1.5 In the event that a national government, after six months, fails to submit the World Constitution for ratification as requested, then the global agency assuming responsibility for the worldwide ratification campaign may proceed to conduct a direct referendum for ratification of the World Constitution by the people. Direct referendums may be organized on the basis of entire nations or countries, or on the basis of existing defined communities within nations.

17.1.6 In the event of a direct ratification referendum, final ratification shall be accomplished by a majority of the votes cast whether for an entire nation or for a World Electoral and Administrative District, provided that ballots are cast by a minimum of twenty-five percent of eligible voters of the area who are over eighteen years of age.

17.1.7 For ratification by existing communities within a nation, the procedure shall be to request local communities, cities, counties, states, provinces, cantons, prefectures, tribal jurisdictions, or other defined political units within a nation to ratify the World Constitution, and to submit the World Constitution for a referendum vote by the citizens of the community or political unit. Ratification may be accomplished by proceeding in this way until all eligible voters of age eighteen and above within the nation or World Electoral and Administrative District have had the opportunity to vote, provided that ballots are cast by a minimum of twenty-five percent of those eligible to vote.

17.1.8 Prior to the Full Operative Stage of World Government, as defined under Section 5 of Article 17, the universities, colleges and scientific academies and institutes in any country may ratify the World Constitution, thus qualifying them for participation in the nomination of Members of the World Parliament to the House of Counsellors.

17.1.9 In the case of those nations currently involved in serious international disputes or where traditional enmities and chronic disputes may exist among two or more nations, a procedure for concurrent paired ratification shall be instituted whereby the nations which are parties to a current or chronic international dispute or conflict may simultaneously ratify the World Constitution. In such cases, the paired nations shall be admitted into the Federation of Earth simultaneously, with the obligation for each such nation to immediately turn over all weapons of mass destruction to the World Government, and to turn over the conflict or dispute for mandatory peaceful settlement by the World Government.

17.1.10 Each nation or political unit which ratifies this World Constitution, either by preliminary ratification or final ratification, shall be bound never to use any armed forces or weapons of mass destruction against another member or unit of the Federation of Earth, regardless of how long it may take to achieve full disarmament of all the nations and political units which ratify this World Constitution.

17.1.11 When ratified, the Constitution for the Federation of Earth becomes the supreme law of Earth. By the act of ratifying this Earth Constitution, any provision in the Constitution or Legislation of any country so ratifying, which is contrary to this Earth Constitution, is either repealed or amended to conform with the Constitution for the Federation of Earth, effective as soon as 25 countries have so ratified. The amendment of National or State Constitutions to allow entry into World Federation is not necessary prior to ratification of the Constitution for the Federation of Earth.

Section 17.2   Stages of Implementation

17.2.1 Implementation of this World Constitution and the establishment of World Government pursuant to the terms of this World Constitution, may be accomplished in three stages, as follows, in addition to the stage of a Provisional World Government as provided under Article 19:

17.2.1.1 First Operative Stage of World Government.

17.2.1.2 Second Operative Stage of World Government.

17.2.1.3 Full Operative Stage of World Government.

17.2.2 At the beginning and during each stage, the World Parliament and the World Executive together shall establish goals and develop means for the progressive implementation of the World Constitution, and for the implementation of legislation enacted by the World Parliament.

Section 17.3   First Operative Stage of World Government

17.3.1 The first operative stage of World Government under this World Constitution shall be implemented when the World Constitution is ratified by a sufficient number of nations and/or people to meet one or the other of the following conditions or equivalent:

17.3.1.1 Preliminary or final ratification by a minimum of twenty-five nations, each having a population of more than 100,000.

17.3.1.2 Preliminary or final ratification by a minimum of ten nations above 100,000 population, together with ratification by direct referendum within a minimum of fifty additional World Electoral and Administrative Districts.

17.3.1.3 Ratification by direct referendum within a minimum of 100 World Electoral and Administrative Districts, even though no nation as such has ratified.

17.3.2 The election of Members of the World Parliament to the House of Peoples shall be conducted in all World Electoral and Administrative Districts where ratification has been accomplished by popular referendum.

17.3.3 The election of Members of the World Parliament to the House of Peoples may proceed concurrently with direct popular referendums both prior to and after the First Operative Stage of World Government is reached.

17.3.4 The appointment or election of Members of the World Parliament to the House of Nations shall proceed in all nations where preliminary ratification has been accomplished.

17.3.5 One-fourth of the Members of the
World Parliament to the House of Counsellors may be elected from nominees submitted by universities and colleges which
have ratified the World Constitution.

17.3.6 The World Presidium and the Executive Cabinet shall be elected according to
the provisions in Article 6, except that
in the absence of a House of Counsellors, the nominations shall be made by
the members of the House of Peoples and
of the House of Nations in joint session.
Until this is accomplished, the Presidium
and Executive Cabinet of the Provisional
World Government as provided in Article
19, shall continue to serve.

17.3.7 When composed, the Presidium for the
first operative stage of World Government
shall assign or re-assign Ministerial posts
among Cabinet and Presidium members,
and shall immediately establish or con-
firm a World Disarmament Agency and a
World Economic and Development Organization.

17.3.8 Those nations which ratify this World
Constitution and thereby join the Federation of Earth, shall immediately transfer all weapons of mass destruction as defined and designated by the World Disar-

mament Agency to that Agency. (See Article 19, Sections A-2-d, B-6 and E-5). The World Disarmament Agency shall immediately immobilize all such weapons and shall proceed with dispatch to dismantle, convert to peacetime use, re-cycle the materials thereof or otherwise destroy all such weapons. During the first operative stage of World Government, the ratifying nations may retain armed forces equipped with weapons other than weapons of mass destruction as defined and designated by the World Disarmament Agency.

17.3.9 Concurrently with the reduction or elimination of such weapons of mass destruction and other military expenditures as can be accomplished during the first operative stage of World Government, the member nations of the Federation of Earth shall pay annually to the Treasury of the World Government amounts equal to one-half the amounts saved from their respective national military budgets during the last year before joining the Federation, and shall continue such payments until the full operative stage of World Government is reached. The World Government shall use fifty percent of the funds thus received to finance the work and projects of the World Economic Development Organization.

17.3.10 The World Parliament and the World Executive shall continue to develop the organs, departments, agencies and activities originated under the Provisional World Government, with such amendments as deemed necessary; and shall proceed to establish and beg in the following organs, departments and agencies of the World Government, if not already underway, together with such other departments, and agencies as are considered desirable and feasible during the first operative stage of World Government:

17.3.10.1 The World Supreme Court;

17.3.10.2 The Enforcement System;

17.3.10.3 The World Ombudsmus;

17.3.10.4 The World Civil Service Administration;

17.3.10.5 The World Financial Administration;

17.3.10.6 The Agency for Research and Planning;

17.3.10.7 The Agency for Technological and Environmental Assessment;

17.3.10.8 An Emergency Earth Rescue Administration, concerned with all aspects of climate change and related factors;

17.3.10.9 An Integrated Global Energy System, based on environmentally safe sources;

17.3.10.10 A World University System, under the Department of Education;

17.3.10.11 A World Corporations Office, under the Department of Commerce and Industry;

17.3.10.12 The World Service Corps;

17.3.10.13 A World Oceans and Seabeds Administration.

17.3.11 At the beginning of the first operative stage, the Presidium in consultation with the Executive Cabinet shall formulate and put forward a proposed program for solving the most urgent world problems currently confronting humanity.

17.3.12 The World Parliament shall proceed to work upon solutions to world problems. The World Parliament and the World Executive working together shall institute through the several organs, departments and agencies of the World Government whatever means shall seem appropriate and feasible to accomplish the implementation and enforcement of world legislation, world law and the World Constitution; and in particular shall take certain decisive actions for the welfare of all people on Earth, applicable throughout the world, including but not limited to the following:

17.3.12.1 Expedite the organization and work of an Emergency Earth Rescue Administration, concerned with all aspects of climate change and climate crises;

17.3.12.2 Expedite the new finance, credit and monetary system, to serve human needs;

17.3.12.3 Expedite an integrated global energy system, utilizing solar energy, hydrogen energy, and other safe and sustainable sources of energy;

17.3.12.4 Push forward a global program for agricultural production to achieve maximum sustained yield under conditions which are ecologically sound;

17.3.12.5 Establish conditions for free trade within the Federation of Earth;

17.3.12.6 Call for and find ways to implement a moratorium on nuclear energy projects until all problems are solved concerning safety, disposal of toxic wastes and the dangers of use

or diversion of materials for the production of nuclear weapons;

17.3.12.7 Outlaw and find ways to completely
terminate the production of nuclear
weapons and all weapons of mass
destruction;

17.3.12.8 Push forward programs to assure adequate and non-polluted water supplies and clean air supplies for everybody on Earth;

17.3.12.9 Push forward a global program to
conserve and re-cycle the resources
of Earth.

17.3.12.10 Develop an acceptable program to
bring population growth under control, especially by raising standards
of living.

Section 17.4 Second Operative Stage of World Government

17.4.1 The second operative stage of World
Government shall be implemented when
fifty percent or more of the nations of
Earth have given either preliminary or
final ratification to this World Constitution, provided that fifty percent of the
total population of Earth is included either within the ratifying nations or within

the ratifying nations together with additional World Electoral and Administrative Districts where people have ratified the World Constitution by direct referendum.

17.4.2 The election and appointment of Members of the World Parliament to the several Houses of the World Parliament shall proceed in the same manner as specified for the first operative stage in Section 3.2, 3.3, 3.4 and 3.5 of Article 17.

17.4.3 The terms of office of the Members of the World Parliament elected or appointed for the first operative stage of World Government, shall be extended into the second operative stage unless they have already served five year terms, in which case new elections or appointments shall be arranged. The terms of holdover Members of the World Parliament into the second operative stage shall be adjusted to run concurrently with the terms of those who are newly elected at the beginning of the second operative stage.

17.4.4 The World Presidium and the Executive Cabinet shall be re-constituted or reconfirmed, as needed, at the beginning of the second operative stage of World Government.

17.4.5 The World Parliament and the World Executive shall continue to develop the organs, departments, agencies and activities which are already underway from the first operative stage of World Government, with such amendments as deemed necessary; and shall proceed to establish and develop all other organs and major departments and agencies of the World Government to the extent deemed feasible during the second operative stage.

17.4.6 All nations joining the Federation of Earth to compose the second operative stage of World Government, shall immediately transfer all weapons of mass destruction and all other military weapons and equipment to the World Disarmament Agency, which shall immediately immobilize such weapons and equipment and shall proceed forthwith to dismantle, convert to peacetime uses, recycle the materials thereof, or otherwise destroy such weapons and equipment. During the second operative stage, all armed forces and para-military forces of the nations which have joined the Federation of Earth shall be completely disarmed and either disbanded or converted on a voluntary basis into elements of the non-military World Service Corps.

17.4.7 Concurrently with the reduction or elimination of such weapons, equipment and other military expenditures as can be accomplished during the second operative stage of World Government, the member nations of the Federation of Earth shall pay annually to the Treasury of the World Government amounts equal to one-half of the amounts saved from their national military budgets during the last year before joining the Federation and shall continue such payments until the full operative stage of World Government is reached. The World Government shall use fifty percent of the funds thus received to finance the work and projects of the World Economic Development Organization.

17.4.8 Upon formation of the Executive Cabinet for the second operative stage, the Presidium shall issue an invitation to the General Assembly of the United Nations Organization and to each of the specialized agencies of the United Nations, as well as to other useful international agencies, to transfer personnel, facilities, equipment, resources and allegiance to the Federation of Earth and to the World Government thereof. The agencies and functions of the United Nations Organization and of its specialized agencies and of other international agencies which may be thus transferred, shall be reconstituted as needed and integrated into the several organs, departments, offices and agencies of the World Government.

17.4.9 Near the beginning of the second operative stage, the Presidium in consultation with the Executive cabinet, shall formulate and put forward a proposed program for solving the most urgent world problems currently confronting the people of Earth.

17.4.10 The World Parliament shall proceed with legislation necessary for implementing a complete program for solving the current urgent world problems.

17.4.11 The World Parliament and the World Executive working together shall develop through the several organs, departments and agencies of the World Government whatever means shall seem appropriate and feasible to implement legislation for solving world problems; and in particular shall take certain decisive actions for the welfare of all people on Earth, including but not limited to the following:

17.4.11.1 Declaring all oceans, seas and canals having supra-national character (but

not including inland seas traditionally belonging to particular nations)
from twenty kilometers offshore, and
all the seabeds thereof, to be under
the ownership of the Federation of
Earth as the common heritage of humanity, and subject to the control
and management of the World Government.

17.4.11.2 Declare the polar caps and surrounding polar areas, including the continent of Antartica but not areas which
are traditionally a part of particular
nations, to be world territory owned
by the Federation of Earth as the
common heritage of humanity, and
subject to control and management
by the World Government.

17.4.11.3 Outlaw the possession, stockpiling,
sale and use of all nuclear weapons,
all weapons of mass destruction,
and all other military weapons and
equipment.

17.4.11.4 Establish an ever-normal grainery
and food supply system for the people of Earth.

17.4.11.5 Develop and carry forward insofar
as feasible all actions defined under
Sec. 3.10, and 3.12 of the First Operative Stage.

Section 17.5   Full Operative Stage of World Government

17.5.1 The full operative stage of World Government shall be implemented when this World Constitution is given either preliminary or final ratification by meeting either condition (17.5.1.1) or (17.5.1.2):

17.5.1.1 Ratification by eighty percent or more of the nations of Earth comprising at least ninety percent of the population of Earth; or

17.5.1.2 Ratification which includes ninety percent of Earth's total population, either within ratifying nations or within ratifying nations together with additional World Electoral and Administrative Districts where ratification by direct referendum has been accomplished, as provided in Article 17, Section 1.

17.5.2 When the full operative stage of World Government is reached, the following conditions shall be implemented:

17.5.2.1 Elections for Members of the House of Peoples shall be conducted in all World Electoral and Administrative Districts where elections have not already taken place; and Members of the House of Nations shall be elected or appointed by the national legislatures or national governments in all nations where this has not already been accomplished.

17.5.2.2 The terms of office for Members of the House of Peoples and of the House of Nations serving during the second operative stage, shall be continued into the full operative stage, except for those who have already served five years, in which case elections shall be held or appointments made as required.

17.5.2.3 The terms of office for all holdover Members of the House of Peoples and of the House of Nations who have served less than five years, shall be adjusted to run concurrently with those Members of the World Parliament whose terms are beginning with the full operative stage.

17.5.2.4 The second 100 Members of the House of Counsellors shall be elected according to the procedure specified in Section 5 of Article 5. The terms of office for holdover Members of the House of Counsellors shall run five more years after the beginning of the full operative stage, while those beginning their terms with the full operative stage shall serve ten years.

17.5.2.5 The Presidium and the Executive Cabinet shall be reconstituted in accordance with the provisions of Article 6.

17.5.2.6 All organs of the World Government shall be made fully operative, and shall be fully developed for the effective administration and implementation of world legislation, world law and the provisions of this World Constitution.

17.5.2.7 All nations which have not already done so shall immediately transfer all military weapons and equipment to the World Disarmament Agency, which shall immediately immobilize all such weapons and shall proceed forthwith to dismantle, convert to peaceful usage, recycle the materials thereof, or otherwise to destroy such weapons and equipment.

17.5.2.8 All armies and military forces of every kind shall be completely disarmed, and either disbanded or converted and integrated on a voluntary basis into the nonmilitary World Service Corps.

17.5.2.9 All viable agencies of the United Nations Organization and other viable international agencies established among national governments, together with their personnel, facilities and resources, shall be transferred to the World Government and reconstituted and integrated as may be useful into the organs, departments, offices, institutes, commissions, bureaus and agencies of the World Government.

17.5.2.10 The World Parliament and the World Executive shall continue to develop the activities and projects which are already underway from the second operative stage of World Government, with such amendments as deemed necessary; and shall proceed with a complete and full scale program to solve world problems and serve the welfare of all people on Earth, in accordance with the provisions of this World Constitution.

Section 17.6   Costs of Ratification

The work and costs of private Citizens of Earth for the achievement of a ratified Constitution for the Federation of Earth, are recognized as legitimate costs for the establishment of constitutional world government by which present and future generations will benefit, and shall be repaid double the original amount by the World Financial Administration of the World Government when it becomes operational after 25 countries have ratified this Constitution for the Federation of Earth. Repayment specifically includes contributions to the World Government Funding Corporation and other costs and expenses recognized by standards and procedures to be established by the World Financial Administration.

Article 18

Amendments

Section 18.1

Following completion of the first operative stage of World Government, amendments to this World Constitution may be proposed for consideration in two ways:

18.1.1 By a simple majority vote of any House of the World Parliament.

18.1.2 By petitions signed by a total of 200,000 persons eligible to vote in world elections from a total of at least twenty World Electoral and Administrative Districts where the World Constitution has received final ratification.

Section 18.2

Passage of any amendment proposed by a
House of the World Parliament shall require an
absolute two-thirds majority vote of each of the
three Houses of the World Parliament voting
separately.

Section 18.3

An amendment proposed by popular petition
shall first require a simple majority vote of the
House of Peoples, which shall be obliged to take
a vote upon the proposed amendment. Passage
of the amendment shall then require an absolute two-thirds majority vote of each of the three
Houses of the World Parliament voting separately.

Section 18.4

Periodically, but no later than ten years after
first convening the World Parliament for the
First Operative Stage of World Government,
and every 20 years thereafter, the Members of
the World Parliament shall meet in special session comprising a Constitutional Convention to
conduct a review of this World Constitution
to consider and propose possible amendments,

which shall then require action as specified in Clause 2 of Article 18 for passage.

Section 18.5

If the First Operative Stage of World Government is not reached by the year 1995, then the Provisional World Parliament, as provided under Article 19, may convene another session of the World Constituent Assembly to review the Constitution for the Federation of Earth and consider possible amendments according to procedure established by the Provisional World Parliament.

Section 18.6

Except by following the amendment procedures specified herein, no part of this World Constitution may be set aside, suspended or subverted, neither for emergencies nor caprice nor convenience.

Article 19

Provisional World Government

Section 19.1 Actions to be Taken by the World Constituent Assembly

Upon adoption of the World Constitution by the World Constituent Assembly, the Assembly and such continuing agency or agencies as it shall designate shall do the following, without being limited thereto:

19.1.1 Issue a Call to all Nations, communities and people of Earth to ratify this World Constitution for World Government.

19.1.2 Establish the following preparatory commissions:

19.1.2.1 Ratification Commission.

19.1.2.2 World Elections Commission.

19.1.2.3 World Development Commission.

19.1.2.4 World Disarmament Commission.

19.1.2.5 World Problems Commission.

19.1.2.6 Nominating Commission.

19.1.2.7 Finance Commission.

19.1.2.8 Peace Research and Education Commission.

19.1.2.9 Special commissions on each of several of the most urgent world problems.

19.1.2.10 Such other commissions as may be deemed desirable in order to proceed with the Provisional World Government.

19.1.3 Convene Sessions of a Provisional World Parliament when feasible under the following conditions:

19.1.3.1 Seek the commitment of 500 or more delegates to attend, representing people in 20 countries from five continents, and having credentials defined by Article 19, Section 3;

19.1.3.2 The minimum funds necessary to organize the sessions of the Provisional World Parliament are either on hand or firmly pledged.

19.1.3.3 Suitable locations are confirmed at least nine months in advance, unless emergency conditions justify shorter advance notice.

Section 19.2   Work of the Preparatory Commissions

19.2.1 The Ratification Commission shall carry out a worldwide campaign for the ratification of the World Constitution, both to obtain preliminary ratification by national governments, including national legislatures, and to obtain final ratification by people, including communities. The ratification commission shall continue its work until the full operative stage of World Government is reached.

19.2.2 The World Elections Commission shall prepare a provisional global map of World Electoral and Administrative Districts and Regions which may be revised during the first or second operative stage of World Government, and shall prepare and proceed with plans to obtain the election of

Members of the World Parliament to the House of Emerging World Law 225 Peoples and to the House of Counsellors. The World Elections Commission shall in due course be converted into the World Boundaries and Elections Administration.

19.2.3 After six months, in those countries where national governments have not responded favorable to the ratification call, the Ratification Commission and the World Elections Commission may proceed jointly to accomplish both the ratification of the World Constitution by direct popular referendum and concurrently the election of Members of the World Parliament.

19.2.4 The Ratification Commission may also submit the World Constitution for ratification by universities and colleges throughout the world.

19.2.5 The World Development Commission shall prepare plans for the creation of a World Economic Development Organization to serve all nations and people ratifying the World Constitution, and in particular less developed countries, to begin functioning when the Provisional World Government is established.

19.2.6 The World Disarmament Commission shall prepare plans for the organization of a World Disarmament Agency, to begin functioning when the Provisional World Government is established.

19.2.7 The World Problems Commission shall prepare an agenda of urgent world problems, with documentation, for possible action by the Provisional World Parliament and Provisional World Government.

19.2.8 The Nominating Commission shall prepare, in advance of convening the Provisional World Parliament, a list of nominees to compose the Presidium and the Executive Cabinet for the Provisional World Government.

19.2.9 The Finance Commission shall work on ways and means for financing the Provisional World Government.

19.2.10 The several commissions on particular world problems shall work on the preparation of proposed world legislation and action on each problem, to present to the Provisional World Parliament when it convenes.

Section 19.3 Composition of the Provisional World Parliament

19.3.1 The Provisional World Parliament shall be composed of the following members:

19.3.1.1 All those who were accredited as delegates to the 1977 and 1991 Sessions of the World Constituent Assembly, as well as to any previous Session of the Provisional World Parliament, and who re-confirm their support for the Constitution for the Federation of Earth, as amended.

19.3.1.2 Persons who obtain the required number of signatures on election petitions, or who are designated by Non-Governmental Organizations which adopt approved resolutions for this purpose, or who are otherwise accredited according to terms specified in Calls which may be issued to convene particular sessions of the Provisional World Parliament.

19.3.1.3 Members of the World Parliament to the House of Peoples who are elected from World Electoral and Administrative Districts up to the time of convening the Provisional World Parliament. Members of the World Parliament elected to the House of Peoples may continue to be added to the Provisional World Parliament until the first operative stage of World Government is reached.

19.3.1.4 Members of the World Parliament to the House of Nations who are elected by national legislatures or appointed by national governments up to the time of convening the Provisional World Parliament. Members of the World Parliament to the House of Nations may continue to be added to the Provisional World Parliament until the first operative stage of World Government is reached.

19.3.1.5 Those universities and colleges which have ratified the World Constitution may nominate persons to serve as Members of the World Parliament to the House of Counsellors. The House of Peoples and House of Nations together may then elect from such nominees up to fifty Members of the World Parliament to serve in the House of Counsellors of the Provisional World Government.

19.3.2 Members of the Provisional World Parliament in categories (1) and (2) as defined above, shall serve only until the first operative stage of World Government is declared, but may be duly elected to continue as Members of the World Parliament during the first operative stage.

Section 19.4   Formation of the Provisional World Executive

19.4.1 As soon as the Provisional World Parliament next convenes, it will elect a new Presidium for the Provisional World Parliament and Provisional World Government from among the nominees submitted by the Nominating Commission.

19.4.2 Members of the Provisional World Presidium shall serve terms of three years, and may be re-elected by the Provisional World Parliament, but in any case shall serve only until the Presidium is elected under the First Operative Stage of World Government.

19.4.3 The Presidium may make additional nominations for the Executive Cabinet.

19.4.4 The Provisional World Parliament shall then elect the members of the Executive Cabinet.

19.4.5 The Presidium shall then assign ministerial posts among the members of the Executive Cabinet and of the Presidium.

19.4.6 When steps (1) through (4) of section 19.4. are completed, the Provisional World Government shall be declared in operation to serve the welfare of humanity.

Section 19.5   First Actions of the Provisional World Government

19.5.1 The Presidium, in consultation with the Executive Cabinet, the commissions on particular world problems and the World Parliament, shall define a program for action on urgent world problems.

19.5.2 The Provisional World Parliament shall go to work on the agenda of world problems, and shall take any and all actions it considers appropriate and feasible, in accordance with the provisions of this World Constitution.

19.5.3 Implementation of and compliance with the legislation enacted by the Provisional World Parliament shall be sought on a voluntary basis in return for the benefits to be realized, while strength of the Provisional World Government is being increased by the progressive ratification of the World Constitution.

19.5.4 Insofar as considered appropriate and feasible, the Provisional World Parliament and Provisional World Executive may undertake some of the actions specified under Section 3.12.of Article 17 for the first operative stage of World Government.

19.5.5 The World Economic Development Organization and the World Disarmament Agency shall be established, for correlated actions.

19.5.6 The World Parliament and the Executive Cabinet of the Provisional World Government shall proceed with the organization of other organs and agencies of the World Government on a provisional basis, insofar as considered desirable and feasible, in particular those specified under Section 3.10. of Article 17.

19.5.7 The several preparatory commissions on urgent world problems may be reconstituted as Administrative Departments of the Provisional World Government.

19.5.8 In all of its work and activities, the Provisional World Government shall function

in accordance with the provisions of this
Constitution for the Federation of Earth.

The predicates of a redeemed World derive from the integrated unity in diversity of the whole: World Peace, Global Justice, Human Rights, Reasonable Prosperity, Ecological Sustainability

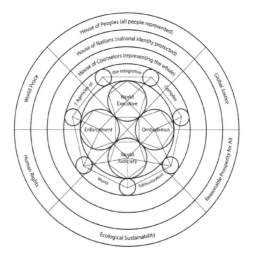

The central agencies of the Federation are structured in terms of councils of five leaders, one from each Continental Division, who rotate as President of their respective agencies. The seven agencies of the Integrative Complex and 28 departments of the World Administration, staffed by professionals in the global civil service, bring order and intelligence into all global processes. The House of Nations, The House of Peoples, and the wise ones in the House of Counselors bring unity in diversity to integrating all nations and peoples and to governing our precious planet Earth.

Signatures

WE strongly believe that the Earth Constitution is entirely adequate for the global legal renaissance of emerging world law. We citizens of the world who have encountered this marvelous document urge the rest of the citizens of our world to seriously consider the value of the Constitutions rapid adoption, so that there is the elevation of democratic self-government to the planetary level. Ratification and implementation of this Constitution will forever put an end to the war system, the poverty system, the exploitation system, and the system of environmental destruction now in place.

On the following pages are the signatures of persons from every walk of life who attended the second and fourth sessions of the World Constituent Assembly, where there were official signing ceremonies, together with a list of persons on the last page who had wanted to attend and who agreed to support the Earth Constitution. Since the time of the official ceremonies, hundreds of thousands more people have signed their support for the document.

Our immediate goal is to get both the joint ratification of a large number of national governments (about 25, perhaps) and also the measured direct ratification by the people of the world adequate to initiate the first operative stage as defined in the Earth Constitution.

Participants in the World Constituent Assembly, 16 to 29 of June, 1977, have affixed their
signatures to the draft of the CONSTITUTION FOR THE FEDERATION OF EARTH herewith:

[signature]   *India*

[signature]   MEXICO

Philip Isely   EARTH, USA

Lucile W. Green   Earth, USA

[signature] Hon. Legal Advisor

Kennibe Newcombe   Canada

T.P. Amerasinghe   Sri Lanka.

[signature]   *Kenya*

Archie Casely Stafford   Ghana.

K. Koma   Botswana

Helen Tucker (Canada) Women's Universal Movement

[signature]   Fed. Rep. of Germany

Thane Read   U.S.A.

[signature] Spencer   India.

Rachoosunah A. Ammujin   Thailand

Rose J. Chesney,   Australia.

[signature]   *[signature]*

[signature]   Netherlands

Joshua [signature]   JAPAN

Andrea von Schmidt — Germany
Edith Barwich — Germany
Greta Gimbel — Germany
Hans Flakus-Schlichtmann — Germany
Ann Mack — World, U.S.A.
Gerald Mack — U.S.A.
Dr. Ludwig Clausing — W.Germany
Dr. Fred Ferd Schlick — U.S.A.
Max Sager — Germany
Helga Mayer — Germany
Beatrice Mayers — U.S.A.
Elisabeth Warenbauer — INNSBRUCK
Thea Feucht — Switzerland
Dr. Helen K. Billings — U.S.A.
Magister Kirsti Poketheyer — Finland, live in Mexico
Robert Rosamund — United People Federation of Earth
Valerie Hagenhuber — Austria
Herbert Gödler

Lois K. Gumley	U.S.A
P. C. Malhotra	India
Hildegard Heuer	Schweiz
PURAN SINGH AZAD	(INDIA)
Dr Miss. Geeta Shah	INDIA.
Maria Freli	Schweiz
Karl Krenting	Innsbruck
Bonnie Allen	U.S.A
Rustom M. Bharucha	India.
Alan Bryant	USA
Jeanne C. Burrows	USA, World
Leo J. Murray sr (Ro Christi USA)	
Simon R Lodi	Botswana
Mrs. Renée Dangoor	United Kingdom
Mh. J. Lelaka	Botswana
Peggy Laine	Australia
Ronald L Palmer	Australia
Tatiana Gulka	AUSTRIA

Dr. Hildegard Dürgen   U.S.A.

Flora Lynne Allen

Samar Basu   India.

Robert W. Kaminski   Earth   USA, Allen Del

Yogi Shantiswarop.   India for one world.

Carmel Kinsman   U.S.A.

Mortimer Lifoly   U.S.A.

D. Hermannes Weaya   Austria

Nina Harada   Canada

Anna Marin   P. R.

Nami Dawgoor   U.K.

Bernadett F. Jonathas.

Andy Ann White Feb D. Ohio U.S.A.

Everett Rafer   Iriad. U.S.A.

Mildred J. Parmelee   U.S.A.

Dr. (Mrs.) Kamoo Patel Pondichery (India)

Margaret Gaspe United Kingdom.

Sri Lanka

U. S. A.

Austria

PUERTO RICO

N.S.A.

Puerto Rico

India.

U. S. A.

Earth !

Denmark

U. S. A.

U.S.A.

Kenya

W- Germany

U.S.A.

Nigeria

JAPAN

Netherlands

Botswana

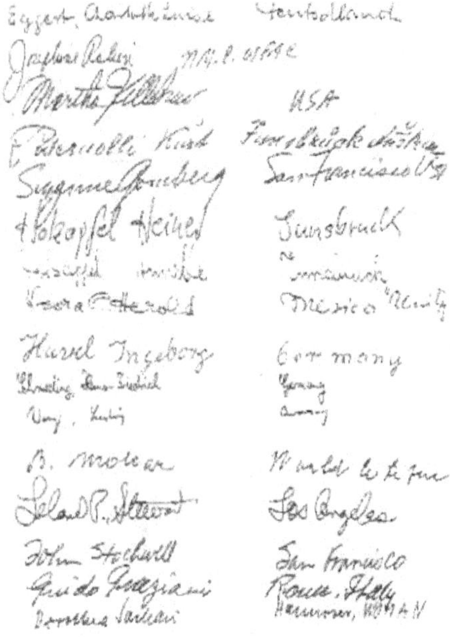
USA
Innsbruck
Harvel Ingeborg
Germany
Los Angeles
San Francisco
Roma, Italy

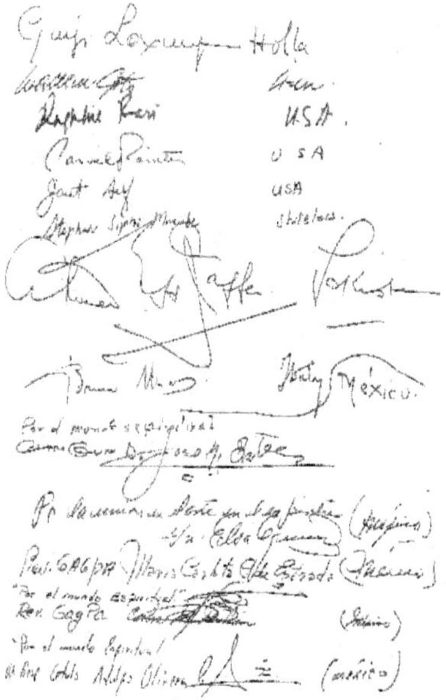
Holla
USA.
U S A
USA
México
Por el mundo espiritual

Signature	Country
Vakoqa Hinge	Mexico
Jifini Hollinger	Austria
[illegible]	Austria
Hubat Ilin	Deutschland (BRD)
Sidbhai Patel	Kenya
Malaben Patel	Indian
Umesh A Patel	Great Britain
Kumud S. Patel	Great Britain.
Ahmed Subanjo q	Indonesia.
[illegible]	Indonesia
Sybil Priest	New Zealand + USA
Alice Stephens	England
Elizabeth E. Stewart	United States
[illegible]	Bangladesh
HARSHA JAY SINGH Khalsa	USA
Sikh Dharma; Washington	

Note: The list of most signers of the CONSTITUTION FOR THE FEDERATION OF EARTH would include several hundred more persons from 31y countries, prevented only by the cost of travel to attend the Assembly at Innsbruck, Austria.

HELD AT TROIA, PORTUGAL, 29th APRIL, TO 9th MAY, 1994

Prof. Dr. Kalman Abraham, Hungary

Atiku Abubakar, Nigeria

Dr. Ebeneezer Ade Adenekan, Nigeria

Malcolm S. Adiseshiah, India

Abdur Rahim Ahamed, Bangladesh

Shahzada/Kabir Ahmed

Mohsin A. Alaini, Yemen

MD. Nurul Alam, U.S.A.

MD. Maher Ali, Bangladesh

Dr. Terence P. Amerasinghe, Sri Lanka

Samir Amin, Senegal

Benjamin K. Amonoo, Ghana

George Anca, Romania

Mauricio Andres-Ribeiro, Brazil

Dr. Munawar A. Anees, U.S.A.

Rev. Ebeneezer Annan, Ivory Coast

Jose Ayala-Lasso, Ecuador

Ir. Hasan Basri, Indonesia

Samar Basu, India

Tony Benn, United Kingdom

Prof. Mrs. Edvige Bestazzi, Italy

Petter Jakob Bjerve, Norway

Goran von Bonsdorff, Finland

Selma Brackman, U.S.A.

Jean-Marie Breton, Int. Regis. World Citizens

Tomas Bruckman, Germany (East)

Dennis Brutus, South Africa (U.S.A.)

Dr. Mihai Titus Carapancea, Romania

Prof. Henri Cartan, France

Amb. Khub Chand, India

Dr. Sripati Chandrasekhar, India

Most Rev. French Chang-Him, Seychelles

Stanyarasal Chinanphra, Zimbabwe

Pratap Chandra Chunder, India

Prof. Dr. Rodney Daniel, France

Daniel G. De Culla, Spain

Dr. Dimitrios S. Delivanis, Greece

Prof. Dr. Francis Dessart, Belgium

Raymond F. Douw, Germany

Prof. Hans-Peter Duerr, Germany

Kennedy Emekam, Nigeria

M. Necati Munir Ertekun, Cyprus

Douglas Niaom Everingham, Australia

John R. Ewbank, U.S.A.

Marjorie Ewbank, U.S.A.

Miss Lissmangi Fanai, India

Dr. Mark Farber, U.S.A.

Fang Ping-Cheng, China

Prof. Dr. Mircea Georghiu, Romania

Lucile W. Green, U.S.A.

Dr. Dauji Gupta, India

Kishelay Gupta, India

Takeshi Haruki, Japan

Dr. Gerhard Herzberg, Canada

Jozsef Horp, Hungary

A. K. Fazlul Hoque, Bangladesh

Choudhury Anwar Hosain, Bangladesh

Margaret Isely, U.S.A. (Earth)

Philip Isely, U.S.A. (Earth)

Ram K. Jiwantolara, Nepal

Roy E. Johnstone, Jamaica

Mohammed Kamaluddin, Bangladesh

Mohammad Rezaul Karim, Bangladesh

Rev. George Karunakaran, India

Dr. Inamullah Khan, Pakistan

Johnson S. Khan, Pakistan

Roger Kotila, Ph.D., U.S.A.

David M. Krieger, U.S.A.

Diemuth Kucbart, Germany

Jul Lag, Norway

Ron M. Leito, Netherlands Antilles

Thomas Lim, East Malaysia

Adam Lopatka, Poland

Anwarul Majid, Bangladesh

Dr. M. Sadiq Malik, Pakistan

Guy Marchand, France

Alvin M. Martin, U.S.A.

Bernardshaw Mazi, Nigeria

Dr. Zhores A. Medvedev, U. K. (USSR)

Anna Medvegyay, Hungary

R. C. Mehrotra, India

Charles Mercieca, U.S.A.

Lt. Col. Pedro B. Merida, Philippines

Yerucham Moshel, Israel

Shete Mikoyelo, Zaire

Mohammed Ebhadine Alli, Switzerland

Rev. Toshio Miyake, Japan

Shettima Ali Monguno CFR
Shettima Ali Monguno, Nigeria

Swapan Mukherjee, India

Hanna Newcombe
Hanna Newcombe, Canada

Srij P.P.Nigam, India

JOSEPHINE OKAFOR.
Josephine Okafor, Nigeria

Johnson Olatunde, Sierra Leone

Rev. Nelson Onono-Onweng, Uganda

Umur Ozturk, Turkey

Yasar Ozturk, Turkey

Linus Pauling, U.S.A.

Fernando Perez Tella, Spain

Emil Otto Peter, Austria

Dr. Alex Quaison-Sackey, Ghana

Sadij Raikkonen, Finland

Sudhir Kumar Rangh, India

Thane Read, U.S.A.

Dr. Sayed Qassem Reshtia, Switzerland

Erzsebet Rethy, Hungary

Miguel S. Ricardo, Portugal

C. Rivas Mijares, Venezuela

Reinhart Ruge, Mexico

Prof. Sir A. M. Sadek, South Africa

Abdus Salam, Italy

Akbar Ali Saleh, Comoros Islands

Blagovest Sendov, Bulgaria

Indira Shrestha, Nepal

Rabi Charan Shrestha, Nepal

Jon Silkin, United Kingdom

Jogel Simsath, Slovak Republic

Dr. Kewal Singh, India

Blanco Sloan, U.S.A.

Ross Smyth, Canada

Lord Donald Soper, United Kingdom

Scott Jefferson Starquester, U.S.A.

Homi J. H. Taleyarkhan, India

Rev. Yoshiaki Toeda, Japan

Dr. Duja K. Torla, Tunisia

Helen Tucker, Canada

Evelyn Utulu, Nigeria

Mrs. Justina N. Uwechue, Nigeria

Ogieva O. Uwaigho, Nigeria

Ann Valentin, U.S.A.

T. Nkuii Pezveqis, U.S.A.

Janjghia Rau 2020 ka 24 Fi
Jorger Lurece Vu, Suan oru

George Walsh
George Walsh, U.S.A.

P. d. DeDi..
Prof. D. A. Plant, United Kingdom

Kavniem X. Clave, U.S.A.

Ban na Aanal-
Raneli Dhops, U.S.A.

New Flannakki Converse

Richard Wilfost
Richard W. Pross, U.S.A.

Alwodin
Dr. Sylvestaar Zawardzki, Poland

Prof. Chief J.O. Agbaye, Nigeria
Dr. Pamela Adewu, Grenada
Sir Abdul W.M. Aowen, Sri Lanka
Ramen Aorool, Palestine
Hon. Lubuer Halen, Poland
Chief Dr. Riskawihe Balogun, Nigeria
Dr. Saburi O. Biobaku, Nigeria
Dr. Jur. Jan Camongerd-x, Slovakia
Dr. Gouin Cadieu, Cote D'Ivoire
Amaranth Chaudhary, India
Abha Justice L. P. Chchoukunde, Zambia
Asha Kumar De, India
Dr. Maulidi El Dossouky, Kuwait
Dr. Rolf Filberg, Sweden
Dr. Benjaman B. Ferener, U.S.A.
Prof. Vitalii I.Goldanskii, Russia
Prof. Dr. Zbigniew Gemyth, Poland
Prof. Errol P. Harris, U.S.A./U.K.
J.R. Jaen Gasacor S. Argentina
Sir Dr. Akura Iuran, Nigeria
K. Jeevagahav, Sri Lanka
R. R. Jasen, India
Dr. Jan Kleinert, Slovakia
Dr. Yuo A. Kranyin, Russia
Adv. Ranjan L.Khanyal, India
Adv. Agil Lodhi, Pakistan
Dr. Nikolai A. Logunkov, Russia
Morksan Lobis, Iran seat
Perry Mauter, Ghana
Kapaan Mekcar, Panama
Dr. Ignacy Malecki, Poland
Prof. Ivan Malek, Czechoslovakia
Dr. Mrs Aita G. Masevich, Russia
Abhtgero S. Muinstuola, Switzerland

Dr. Milenko Mihajlov, Yugoslavia
Hon. Ram Niwas Mirdha, India
Dr. Ruben Muller, Costa Rica
Justice M. A. Muttaith, Bangladesh
Dr. Sdeke G. Mwale, Zambia
Dr. Rashmi Mayor, India
Dr. Jayan. V. Narihar, India
Paul Niladi, Nigeria
Osman.N. Orek, Turkish Rep. N. Cyprus
Prof. Lenard Pal, Poland
Prof. Jean-Claude Pecker, France
Prof. Gamios T. Peiris, Sri Lanka
Gerard Piel, U.S.A.
Rev. Daniel O. Pupiah, Cote D'Ivoire
Prof. M. S. Rajan, India
Prof. C. N. R. Rau, India
Sri N. S. Rau, India
Michel Rocrank, Poland
Dr. Frederick Sanger, U. K.
Sir Ainsworth D. Rom, Jamaica
David Shahar, Israel
Tomu Sik, Israel
Chandan Sem, India
Hon. Robert D. G. Stanbury, Canada
Dr. Bogdan Suchodolski, Poland
Abdul Lodhy Sulaiman, Sri Lanka
Dr. Sol Tax, U.S.A.
Mallaxmi Obenawan Terry, Ghana
Dr. Walter R. Thirrint, Austria
Most Rev. Desmond M. Tutu, South Africa
Kenji Urata, Japan
Dr. Pieter Van Dijk, Netherlands
Csaba Worter, M.D., U.S.A.
Rod Welford, M.L.A., Australia

A Pledge of Allegiance
to the Earth Constitution

I pledge allegiance to the Constitution for the Federation of Earth, and to the Republic of free world citizens for which it stands,

One Earth Federation, protecting by law the rich diversity of the Earths citizens, One Earth Federation, protecting the precious ecology of our planet.

I pledge allegiance to the World Parliament representing all nations and peoples, and to the democratic processes by which it proceeds,

One law for the Earth, with freedom and equality for all, One standard of justice, with a bill of rights protecting each.

I pledge allegiance to the future generations protected by the Earth Constitution, And to the unity, integrity, and beauty of humankind, living in harmony on the Earth,

One Earth Federation, conceived in love, truth, and hope, with peace and prosperity for all.

World Constitution and Parliament Association (WCPA)

Sponsor for the Earth Constitution and the Provisional World Parliament At the heart of the global Earth Federation Movement

President: Dr. Glen T. Martin, USA
wcpaorg@gmail.com

Secretary General: Dr. Eugenia Almand, USA

In cooperation with:

Earth Federation Institute (EFI)

(formerly Institute on World Problems (IOWP))

A 501(c)(3) tax deductible organization
313 Seventh Ave., Radford, VA 24141, USA

Treasurer: Phyllis Turk, MS, CNM:
phyllisturk@wcpa-org.us

www.earth-constitution.org
(sign up for WCPA at the above url)
www.worldparliament-gov.org
www.earthfederation.info
www.earthfederationinstitute.org

Offering World Citizen voter registration ID cards

Offering seminars and lectures worldwide

Offering a chance to be involved
for a liberated human future

Organizing chapters and communications
in countries worldwide

CPSIA information can be obtained
at www.ICGtesting.com
Printed in the USA
BVHW092253060220
571640BV00005B/212